www.EffortlessMath.com

... So Much More Online!

✓ FREE Math lessons

✓ More Math learning books!

✓ Mathematics Worksheets

✓ Online Math Tutors

Need a PDF version of this book?

Visit www.EffortlessMath.com

SSAT Lower Level Math Exercise Book

Student Workbook and Two Realistic

SSAT Lower Level Math Tests

By

Reza Nazari & Ava Ross

Copyright © 2019

Reza Nazari & Ava Ross

All inquiries should be addressed to:

info@EffortlessMath.com

www.EffortlessMath.com

ISBN-13: 978-1-970036-44-2

ISBN-10: 1-970036-44-3

Published by: Effortless Math Education

www.EffortlessMath.com

Description

Get ready for the SSAT Lower Level Math Test with a PERFECT Math Workbook!

SSAT Lower Level Math Exercise book, which reflects the 2019 test guidelines and topics, is dedicated to preparing test takers to ace the SSAT Lower Level Math Test. This SSAT Lower Level Math workbook's new edition has been updated to replicate questions appearing on the most recent SSAT Lower Level Math tests. Here is intensive preparation for the SSAT Lower Level Math test, and a precious learning tool for test takers who need extra practice in math to raise their SSAT Lower Level Math scores. After completing this workbook, you will have solid foundation and adequate practice that is necessary to ace the SSAT Lower Level Math test. **This workbook is your ticket to score higher on SSAT Lower Level Math.**

The updated version of this hands-on workbook represents extensive exercises, math problems, sample SSAT Lower Level questions, and quizzes with answers and detailed solutions to help you hone your math skills, overcome your exam anxiety, and boost your confidence -- and do your best to defeat SSAT Lower Level exam on test day.

Each of math exercises is answered in the book and we have provided explanation of the answers for the two full-length SSAT Lower Level Math practice tests as well which will help test takers find their weak areas and raise their scores. This is a unique and perfect practice book to beat the SSAT Lower Level Math Test.

Separate math chapters offer a complete review of the SSAT Lower Level Math test, including:

- ✓ Arithmetic and Number Operations
- ✓ Algebra and Functions,
- ✓ Geometry and Measurement
- ✓ Data analysis, Statistics, & Probability
- ✓ … and also includes **two full-length practice tests!**

The surest way to succeed on SSAT Lower Level Math Test is with intensive practice in every math topic tested--and that's what you will get in *SSAT Lower Level Math Exercise Book.* Each chapter of this focused format has a comprehensive review created by Test Prep experts that goes into detail to cover all of the content likely to appear on the SSAT Lower Level Math test. Not only does this all-inclusive workbook offer everything you will ever need to conquer SSAT Lower Level Math test, it also contains two full-length and realistic SSAT Lower Level Math tests that reflect the format and question types on the SSAT Lower Level to help you check your exam-readiness and identify where you need more practice.

Effortless Math Workbook for the *SSAT Lower Level Test* contains many exciting and unique features to help you improve your test scores, including:

- ✓ Content 100% aligned with the 2019 SSAT Lower Level test
- ✓ Written by SSAT Lower Level Math tutors and test experts
- ✓ Complete coverage of all SSAT Lower Level Math concepts and topics which you will be tested
- ✓ Over 2,500 additional SSAT Lower Level math practice questions in both multiple-choice and grid-in formats with answers grouped by topic, so you can focus on your weak areas
- ✓ Abundant Math skill building exercises to help test-takers approach different question types that might be unfamiliar to them
- ✓ Exercises on different SSAT Lower Level Math topics such as integers, percent, equations, polynomials, exponents and radicals
- ✓ 2 full-length practice tests (featuring new question types) with detailed answers

This SSAT Lower Level Math Workbook and other Effortless Math Education books are used by thousands of students each year to help them review core content areas, brush-up in math, discover their strengths and weaknesses, and achieve their best scores on the SSAT Lower Level test.

Do NOT take the SSAT Lower Level test without reviewing the Math questions in this workbook!

About the Author

Reza Nazari is the author of more than 100 Math learning books including:
– **Math and Critical Thinking Challenges:** For the Middle and High School Student
– **ACT Math in 30 Days.**
– **ASVAB Math Workbook 2018 – 2019**
– **Effortless Math Education Workbooks**
– **and many more Mathematics books …**

Reza is also an experienced Math instructor and a test–prep expert who has been tutoring students since 2008. Reza is the founder of Effortless Math Education, a tutoring company that has helped many students raise their standardized test scores—and attend the colleges of their dreams. Reza provides an individualized custom learning plan and the personalized attention that makes a difference in how students view math.

You can contact Reza via email at:
reza@EffortlessMath.com

Find Reza's professional profile at:
goo.gl/zoC9rJ

Contents

Chapter 1: Place Vales and Number Sense

Topics that you'll practice in this chapter:

✓ Place Values

✓ Compare Numbers

✓ Numbers in Numbers

✓ Rounding

✓ Odd or Even

Place Values

✍ *Write numbers in expanded form.*

1) Thirty–five $30 + 5$

2) Sixty–seven   ___ + ___

3) Forty–two   ___ + ___

4) Eighty–nine   ___ + ___

5) Ninety–one   ___ + ___

6) Twenty–two   ___ + ___

7) Thirty–four   ___ + ___

8) Fifty–six   ___ + ___

9) Ninety–five   ___ + ___

10) Seventy–seven   ___ + ___

11) Forty–eight   ___ + ___

✍ *Circle the correct choice.*

12)	The 2 in 72 is in the	ones place	tens place	hundreds place
13)	The 6 in 65 is in the	ones place	tens place	hundreds place
14)	The 2 in 342 is in the	ones place	tens place	hundreds place
15)	The 5 in 450 is in the	ones place	tens place	hundreds place
16)	The 3 in 321 is in the	ones place	tens place	hundreds place

Comparing and Ordering Numbers

✍ *Use less than, equal to or greater than.*

1) 23 _____ 34

2) 89 _____ 98

3) 45 _____ 25

4) 34 _____ 32

5) 91 _____ 91

6) 57 _____ 55

7) 85 _____ 78

8) 56 _____ 43

9) 34 _____ 34

10) 92 _____ 98

11) 38 _____ 46

12) 67 _____ 58

13) 88 _____ 69

14) 23 _____ 34

✍ *Order each set of integers from least to greatest.*

15) $7, -9, -6, -1, 3$ ___, ___, ___, ___, ___, ___

16) $-4, -11, 5, 12, 9$ ___, ___, ___, ___, ___, ___

17) $18, -12, -19, 21, -20$ ___, ___, ___, ___, ___, ___

18) $-15, -25, 18, -7, 32$ ___, ___, ___, ___, ___, ___

19) $37, -42, 28, -11, 34$ ___, ___, ___, ___, ___, ___

20) $78, 46, -19, 77, -24$ ___, ___, ___, ___, ___, ___

✍ *Order each set of integers from greatest to least.*

21) $11, 16, -9, -12, -4$ ___, ___, ___, ___, ___, ___

22) $23, 31, -14, -20, 39$ ___, ___, ___, ___, ___, ___

23) $45, -21, -18, 55, -5$ ___, ___, ___, ___, ___, ___

24) $68, 81, -14, -10, 94$ ___, ___, ___, ___, ___, ___

25) $-5, 69, -12, -43, 34$ ___, ___, ___, ___, ___, ___

26) $-56, -25, -30, 18, 29$ ___, ___, ___, ___, ___, ___

Write Numbers in Words

✎ *Write each number in words.*

1) 194 _____

2) 311 _____

3) 256 _____

4) 434 _____

5) 809 _____

6) 730 _____

7) 272 _____

8) 266 _____

9) 902 _____

10) 1,418 _____

11) 1,365 _____

12) 3,374 _____

13) 2,486 _____

14) 7,671 _____

15) 6,290 _____

16) 3,147 _____

17) 5,012 _____

Rounding Numbers

✎ *Round each number to the nearest ten.*

1) 24	5) 11	9) 47
2) 98	6) 35	10) 63
3) 41	7) 84	11) 79
4) 26	8) 70	12) 55

✎ *Round each number to the nearest hundred.*

13) 185	17) 222	21) 670
14) 254	18) 311	22) 563
15) 729	19) 287	23) 890
16) 109	20) 927	24) 479

✎ *Round each number to the nearest thousand.*

25) 1,252	31) 31,422
26) 1,950	32) 12,723
27) 5,235	33) 61,670
28) 3,567	34) 71,290
29) 8,027	35) 50,930
30) 52,512	36) 38,568

Odd or Even

✍ *Identify whether each number is even or odd.*

1) 12 _____

2) 7 _____

3) 33 _____

4) 18 _____

5) 99 _____

6) 55 _____

7) 34 _____

8) 87 _____

9) 94 _____

10) 14 _____

11) 22 _____

12) 79 _____

✍ *Circle the even number in each group.*

13) 22, 11, 57, 13, 19, 47

14) 15, 17, 27, 23, 33, 26

15) 19, 35, 24, 57, 65, 49

16) 67, 58, 89, 63, 27, 63

✍ *Circle the odd number in each group.*

17) 12, 14, 22, 64, 53, 98

18) 16, 26, 28, 44, 62, 73

19) 46, 82, 63, 98, 64, 56

20) 27, 92, 58, 36, 38, 72

Answers of Worksheets – Chapter 1

Place Values

1) 30 + 5
2) 60 + 7
3) 40 + 2
4) 80 + 9
5) 90 + 1
6) 20 + 2

7) 30 + 4
8) 50 + 6
9) 90 + 5
10) 70 + 7
11) 40 + 8
12) ones place

13) tens place
14) ones place
15) tens place
16) hundreds place

Comparing and Ordering Numbers

1) 23 less than 34

2) 89 less than 98

3) 45 greater than 25

4) 34 greater than 32

5) 91 equals to 91

6) 57 greater than 55

7) 85 greater than 78

8) 56 greater than 43

9) 34 equals to 34

10) 92 less than 98

11) 38 less than 46

12) 67 greater than 58

13) 88 greater than 69

14) 23 less than 34

15) $-9, -6, -1, 3, 7$

16) $-11, -4, 5, 9, 12$

17) $-20, -19, -12, 18, 21$

18) $-25, -15, -7, 18, 32$

19) $-42, -11, 28, 34, 37$

20) $-24, -19, 46, 77, 78$

21) $16, 11, -4, -9, -12$

22) $39, 31, 23, -14, -20$

23) $55, 45, -5, -18, -21$

24) $94, 81, 68, -10, -14$

25) $69, 34, -5, -12, -43$

26) $29, 18, -25, -30, -56$

Word Names for Numbers

1) one hundred ninety-four

2) three hundred eleven

3) two hundred fifty-six

4) four hundred thirty-four

5) eight hundred nine

6) seven hundred thirty

7) two hundred seventy-two

8) two hundred sixty-six

9) nine hundred two

10) one thousand, four hundred eighteen

11) one thousand, three hundred sixty-five

12) three thousand, three hundred seventy-four

13) two thousand, four hundred eighty-six

14) seven thousand, six hundred seventy-one

15) six thousand, two hundred ninety

16) three thousand, one hundred forty-seven

17) five thousand, twelve

Rounding Numbers

1) 20	13) 200	25) 1,000
2) 100	14) 300	26) 2,000
3) 40	15) 700	27) 5,000
4) 30	16) 100	28) 4,000
5) 10	17) 200	29) 8,000
6) 40	18) 300	30) 53,000
7) 80	19) 300	31) 31,000
8) 70	20) 900	32) 13,000
9) 50	21) 700	33) 62,000
10) 60	22) 600	34) 71,000
11) 80	23) 900	35) 51,000
12) 60	24) 500	36) 39,000

Odd or Even

1) even	8) odd	15) 24
2) odd	9) even	16) 58
3) odd	10) even	17) 53
4) even	11) even	18) 73
5) odd	12) odd	19) 63
6) odd	13) 22	20) 27
7) even	14) 26	

Chapter 2:
Adding and Subtracting

Topics that you'll practice in this chapter:

- ✓ Adding Two–Digit Numbers
- ✓ Subtracting Two–Digit Numbers
- ✓ Adding Three–Digit Numbers
- ✓ Adding Hundreds
- ✓ Adding 4–Digit Numbers
- ✓ Subtracting 4–Digit Numbers

Adding Two–Digit Numbers

✎ *Find each sum.*

1) $\begin{array}{r} 50 \\ + \ 18 \\ \hline \end{array}$

2) $\begin{array}{r} 32 \\ + \ 14 \\ \hline \end{array}$

3) $\begin{array}{r} 45 \\ + \ 16 \\ \hline \end{array}$

4) $\begin{array}{r} 12 \\ + \ 12 \\ \hline \end{array}$

5) $\begin{array}{r} 43 \\ + \ 30 \\ \hline \end{array}$

6) $\begin{array}{r} 34 \\ + \ 15 \\ \hline \end{array}$

7) $\begin{array}{r} 89 \\ + \ \ 7 \\ \hline \end{array}$

8) $\begin{array}{r} 63 \\ + \ 12 \\ \hline \end{array}$

9) $\begin{array}{r} 90 \\ + \ 10 \\ \hline \end{array}$

10) $\begin{array}{r} 24 \\ + \ 12 \\ \hline \end{array}$

11) $\begin{array}{r} 42 \\ + \ 22 \\ \hline \end{array}$

12) $\begin{array}{r} 23 \\ + \ 18 \\ \hline \end{array}$

13) $\begin{array}{r} 18 \\ + \ 25 \\ \hline \end{array}$

14) $\begin{array}{r} 37 \\ + \ 23 \\ \hline \end{array}$

15) $\begin{array}{r} 56 \\ + \ 35 \\ \hline \end{array}$

16) $\begin{array}{r} 65 \\ + \ 40 \\ \hline \end{array}$

17) $\begin{array}{r} 77 \\ + \ 29 \\ \hline \end{array}$

18) $\begin{array}{r} 59 \\ + \ 26 \\ \hline \end{array}$

Subtracting Two-Digit Numbers

✎ *Find each difference.*

1) $\begin{array}{r} 32 \\ -15 \\ \hline \end{array}$

2) $\begin{array}{r} 40 \\ -12 \\ \hline \end{array}$

3) $\begin{array}{r} 67 \\ -17 \\ \hline \end{array}$

4) $\begin{array}{r} 18 \\ -10 \\ \hline \end{array}$

5) $\begin{array}{r} 59 \\ -16 \\ \hline \end{array}$

6) $\begin{array}{r} 89 \\ -20 \\ \hline \end{array}$

7) $\begin{array}{r} 78 \\ -21 \\ \hline \end{array}$

8) $\begin{array}{r} 66 \\ -15 \\ \hline \end{array}$

9) $\begin{array}{r} 87 \\ -45 \\ \hline \end{array}$

10) $\begin{array}{r} 56 \\ -19 \\ \hline \end{array}$

11) $\begin{array}{r} 62 \\ -23 \\ \hline \end{array}$

12) $\begin{array}{r} 47 \\ -20 \\ \hline \end{array}$

13) $\begin{array}{r} 78 \\ -29 \\ \hline \end{array}$

14) $\begin{array}{r} 49 \\ -36 \\ \hline \end{array}$

15) $\begin{array}{r} 82 \\ -38 \\ \hline \end{array}$

16) $\begin{array}{r} 97 \\ -45 \\ \hline \end{array}$

17) $\begin{array}{r} 89 \\ -57 \\ \hline \end{array}$

18) $\begin{array}{r} 95 \\ -73 \\ \hline \end{array}$

Adding Three–Digit Numbers

✎ *Find each sum.*

1)
$$\begin{array}{r} 234 \\ +\ 56 \\ \hline \end{array}$$

2)
$$\begin{array}{r} 523 \\ +\ 134 \\ \hline \end{array}$$

3)
$$\begin{array}{r} 345 \\ +\ 167 \\ \hline \end{array}$$

4)
$$\begin{array}{r} 460 \\ +\ 120 \\ \hline \end{array}$$

5)
$$\begin{array}{r} 432 \\ +\ 430 \\ \hline \end{array}$$

6)
$$\begin{array}{r} 235 \\ +\ 150 \\ \hline \end{array}$$

7)
$$\begin{array}{r} 789 \\ +\ 57 \\ \hline \end{array}$$

8)
$$\begin{array}{r} 863 \\ +\ 340 \\ \hline \end{array}$$

9)
$$\begin{array}{r} 956 \\ +\ 89 \\ \hline \end{array}$$

10)
$$\begin{array}{r} 235 \\ +\ 112 \\ \hline \end{array}$$

11)
$$\begin{array}{r} 156 \\ +\ 117 \\ \hline \end{array}$$

12)
$$\begin{array}{r} 278 \\ +\ 190 \\ \hline \end{array}$$

13)
$$\begin{array}{r} 345 \\ +\ 125 \\ \hline \end{array}$$

14)
$$\begin{array}{r} 420 \\ +\ 120 \\ \hline \end{array}$$

15)
$$\begin{array}{r} 575 \\ +\ 234 \\ \hline \end{array}$$

16)
$$\begin{array}{r} 489 \\ +\ 354 \\ \hline \end{array}$$

17)
$$\begin{array}{r} 621 \\ +\ 213 \\ \hline \end{array}$$

18)
$$\begin{array}{r} 683 \\ +\ 293 \\ \hline \end{array}$$

Adding Hundreds

✎ *Add.*

1) $100 + 100 = ---$

2) $100 + 200 = ---$

3) $200 + 200 = ---$

4) $300 + 200 = ---$

5) $100 + 300 = ---$

6) $200 + 400 = ---$

7) $400 + 100 = ---$

8) $500 + 200 = ---$

9) $300 + 500 = ---$

10) $400 + 700 = ---$

11) $400 + 600 = ---$

12) $500 + 400 = ---$

13) $900 + 100 = ---$

14) $100 + 700 = ---$

15) $500 + 100 = ---$

16) $200 + 800 = ---$

17) $800 + 100 = ---$

18) $700 + 100 = ---$

19) $100 + 300 = ---$

20) $500 + 500 = ---$

21) $400 + 400 = ---$

22) $300 + 400 = ---$

23) $500 + 700 = ---$

24) $800 + 600 = ---$

25) If there are 600 balls in a box and Jackson puts 500 more balls inside, how many balls are in the box?

_____ balls

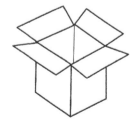

Adding 4–Digit Numbers

✍ *Add.*

1)
$$\begin{array}{r} 1,158 \\ + 6,687 \\ \hline \end{array}$$

4)
$$\begin{array}{r} 3,239 \\ +2,562 \\ \hline \end{array}$$

7)
$$\begin{array}{r} 3,119 \\ +1,245 \\ \hline \end{array}$$

2)
$$\begin{array}{r} 5,188 \\ + 1,298 \\ \hline \end{array}$$

5)
$$\begin{array}{r} 4,257 \\ +5,194 \\ \hline \end{array}$$

8)
$$\begin{array}{r} 5,320 \\ +2,765 \\ \hline \end{array}$$

3)
$$\begin{array}{r} 5,756 \\ + 2,712 \\ \hline \end{array}$$

6)
$$\begin{array}{r} 6,215 \\ +2,189 \\ \hline \end{array}$$

9)
$$\begin{array}{r} 4,890 \\ +4,567 \\ \hline \end{array}$$

✍ *Find the missing numbers.*

7) $1,145 + \underline{\quad} = 1,276$

10) $455 + \underline{\quad} = 1,755$

8) $500 + 1,000 = \underline{\quad}$

11) $\underline{\quad} + 720 = 1,250$

9) $3,200 + \underline{\quad} = 4,300$

12) $\underline{\quad} + 670 = 2,230$

✍ *Solve.*

13) David sells gems. He finds a diamond in Istanbul and buys it for $3,433. Then, he flies to Cairo and purchases a bigger diamond for the bargain price of $5,922. How much does David spend on the two diamonds? _____

Subtracting 4–Digit Numbers

✏ **Subtract.**

1) $\begin{array}{r} 2{,}230 \\ -\ 1{,}112 \\ \hline \end{array}$

4) $\begin{array}{r} 8{,}519 \\ -\ 5{,}422 \\ \hline \end{array}$

7) $\begin{array}{r} 8{,}756 \\ -\ 6{,}712 \\ \hline \end{array}$

2) $\begin{array}{r} 3{,}115 \\ -\ 1{,}980 \\ \hline \end{array}$

5) $\begin{array}{r} 6{,}222 \\ -\ 4{,}331 \\ \hline \end{array}$

8) $\begin{array}{r} 9{,}290 \\ -\ 3{,}829 \\ \hline \end{array}$

3) $\begin{array}{r} 4{,}976 \\ -\ 2{,}678 \\ \hline \end{array}$

6) $\begin{array}{r} 7{,}821 \\ -\ 3{,}212 \\ \hline \end{array}$

9) $\begin{array}{r} 5{,}117 \\ -4{,}216 \\ \hline \end{array}$

✏ **Find the missing number.**

7) $2223 - \underline{\quad} = 1120$

10) $2300 - \underline{\quad} = 1250$

8) $3574 - \underline{\quad} = 2245$

11) $3780 - 1890 = \underline{\quad}$

9) $1124 - 578 = \underline{\quad}$

12) $2880 - 2560 = \underline{\quad}$

✏ **Solve.**

13) Jackson had $3,963 invested in the stock market until he lost $2,171 on those investments. How much money does he have in the stock market now?

Answers of Worksheets – Chapter 2

Adding two–digit numbers

1) 68
2) 46
3) 61
4) 24
5) 73
6) 49

7) 96
8) 75
9) 100
10) 36
11) 64
12) 41

13) 43
14) 60
15) 91
16) 105
17) 106
18) 85

Subtracting two–digit numbers

1) 17
2) 28
3) 50
4) 8
5) 43
6) 69

7) 57
8) 51
9) 42
10) 37
11) 39
12) 27

13) 49
14) 13
15) 44
16) 52
17) 32
18) 22

Adding three–digit numbers

1) 290
2) 657
3) 512
4) 580
5) 862
6) 385

7) 846
8) 1,203
9) 1,045
10) 347
11) 273
12) 468
13) 470

14) 540
15) 809
16) 843
17) 834
18) 976

Adding hundreds

1) 200
2) 300
3) 400
4) 500
5) 400
6) 600
7) 500
8) 700
9) 800

10) 1,100
11) 1,000
12) 900
13) 1,000
14) 800
15) 600
16) 1,000
17) 900
18) 800

19) 400
20) 1,000
21) 800
22) 700
23) 1,200
24) 1,400
25) 1,100

Adding 4–digit numbers

1) 7,845
2) 6,486
3) 8,468
4) 5,801
5) 9,451
6) 8,404

7) 4,364
8) 8,085
9) 9,457
10) 131
11) 1,500
12) 1,100

13) 1,300
14) 530
15) 1,560
16) $9,355

Subtracting 4–digit numbers

1) 1,118
2) 1,135
3) 2,298
4) 3,097
5) 1,891
6) 4,609

7) 2,044
8) 5,461
9) 901
10) 1,103
11) 1,329
12) 546

13) 1,050
14) 1,890
15) 320
16) 1,792

Chapter 3: Multiplication and Division

Topics that you'll practice in this chapter:

✓ Multiplication

✓ Division

✓ Long Division by One Digit

✓ Division with Remainders

Multiplication

✍ *Find the answers.*

1) $\begin{array}{r} 45 \\ \times\ 13 \\ \hline \\ \hline \end{array}$

2) $\begin{array}{r} 32 \\ \times\ 10 \\ \hline \\ \hline \end{array}$

3) $\begin{array}{r} 19 \\ \times\ 12 \\ \hline \\ \hline \end{array}$

4) $\begin{array}{r} 25 \\ \times\ 15 \\ \hline \\ \hline \end{array}$

5) $\begin{array}{r} 38 \\ \times\ 14 \\ \hline \\ \hline \end{array}$

6) $\begin{array}{r} 34 \\ \times\ 24 \\ \hline \\ \hline \end{array}$

7) $\begin{array}{r} 52 \\ \times\ 11 \\ \hline \\ \hline \end{array}$

8) $\begin{array}{r} 47 \\ \times\ 20 \\ \hline \\ \hline \end{array}$

9) $\begin{array}{r} 120 \\ \times\ 9 \\ \hline \\ \hline \end{array}$

10) $\begin{array}{r} 563 \\ \times\ 4 \\ \hline \\ \hline \end{array}$

11) $\begin{array}{r} 365 \\ \times\ 5 \\ \hline \\ \hline \end{array}$

12) $\begin{array}{r} 89 \\ \times\ 25 \\ \hline \\ \hline \end{array}$

13) $\begin{array}{r} 478 \\ \times\ 34 \\ \hline \\ \hline \end{array}$

14) $\begin{array}{r} 956 \\ \times\ 26 \\ \hline \\ \hline \end{array}$

15) $\begin{array}{r} 391 \\ \times\ 78 \\ \hline \\ \hline \end{array}$

16) The Haunted House Ride runs 5 times a day. It has 6 cars, each of which can hold 4 people. How many people can ride the Haunted House Ride in one day?

17) Each train car has 3 rows of seats. There are 4 seats in each row. How many seats are there in 5 train cars?

Division

✍ *Find each missing number.*

1) $8 \div \underline{\quad} = 4$

2) $\underline{\quad} \div 4 = 3$

3) $14 \div \underline{\quad} = 2$

4) $\underline{\quad} \div 5 = 3$

5) $18 \div \underline{\quad} = 2$

6) $\underline{\quad} \div 7 = 3$

7) $10 \div \underline{\quad} = 1$

8) $48 \div 12 = \underline{\quad}$

9) $99 \div \underline{\quad} = 9$

10) $70 \div 10 = \underline{\quad}$

11) $44 \div \underline{\quad} = 4$

12) $24 \div \underline{\quad} = 2$

13) $\underline{\quad} \div 10 = 4$

14) $110 \div 11 = \underline{\quad}$

15) $12 \div \underline{\quad} = 1$

16) $90 \div \underline{\quad} = 9$

17) $\underline{\quad} \div 11 = 8$

18) $\underline{\quad} \div 12 = 11$

19) $60 \div \underline{\quad} = 6$

20) $\underline{\quad} \div 11 = 12$

21) $84 \div 12 = \underline{\quad}$

22) $80 \div 10 = \underline{\quad}$

23) $11 \div 11 = \underline{\quad}$

24) $144 \div \underline{\quad} = 12$

✍ *Solve.*

25) Anna has 120 books. She wants to put them in equal numbers on 12 bookshelves. How many books can she put on a bookshelf?   _____ books

26) If dividend is 99 and the quotient is 11, then what is the divisor? _____

27) Emily has 64 fruit juice that she would like to give to her 8 friends. If she shares them equally, how many fruit juice will she give to each? _____ fruit juice

Long Division by One Digit

✐ *Find the quotient.*

1) $8\overline{)40}$ =

2) $5\overline{)30}$ =

3) $6\overline{)36}$ =

4) $4\overline{)40}$ =

5) $6\overline{)42}$ =

6) $8\overline{)64}$ =

7) $7\overline{)35}$ =

8) $7\overline{)49}$ =

9) $8\overline{)56}$ =

10) $9\overline{)36}$ =

11) $7\overline{)28}$ =

12) $8\overline{)32}$ =

13) $8\overline{)72}$ =

14) $7\overline{)70}$ =

15) $6\overline{)54}$ =

16) $11\overline{)99}$ =

17) $12\overline{)144}$ =

18) $5\overline{)60}$ =

19) $6\overline{)84}$ =

20) $7\overline{)112}$ =

21) $8\overline{)152}$ =

22) $8\overline{)168}$ =

23) $7\overline{)819}$ =

24) $5\overline{)225}$ =

25) $6\overline{)792}$ =

26) $5\overline{)350}$ =

27) $6\overline{)174}$ =

28) $8\overline{)104}$ =

29) $3\overline{)102}$ =

30) $9\overline{)189}$ =

31) $5\overline{)115}$ =

32) $2\overline{)120}$ =

33) $7\overline{)112}$ =

34) $4\overline{)148}$ =

35) $9\overline{)126}$ =

36) $6\overline{)240}$ =

37) $4\overline{)576}$ =

38) $4\overline{)512}$ =

39) $9\overline{)1278}$ =

40) $8\overline{)2768}$ =

41) $6\overline{)1224}$ =

42) $4\overline{)3412}$ =

Division with Remainders

✍ *Find the quotient with remainder.*

1) $5\overline{)27}$

2) $2\overline{)19}$

3) $4\overline{)17}$

4) $7\overline{)23}$

5) $6\overline{)34}$

6) $5\overline{)41}$

7) $5\overline{)26}$

8) $7\overline{)29}$

9) $4\overline{)33}$

10) $7\overline{)46}$

11) $8\overline{)59}$

12) $8\overline{)67}$

13) $9\overline{)65}$

14) $7\overline{)50}$

15) $9\overline{)84}$

16) $9\overline{)95}$

17) $4\overline{)85}$

18) $7\overline{)93}$

19) $8\overline{)117}$

20) $5\overline{)124}$

21) $8\overline{)189}$

22) $7\overline{)256}$

23) $4\overline{)265}$

24) $6\overline{)232}$

25) $5\overline{)592}$

26) $3\overline{)295}$

27) $6\overline{)553}$

28) $5\overline{)214}$

29) $3\overline{)440}$

30) $7\overline{)673}$

31) $4\overline{)213}$

32) $2\overline{)820}$

33) $5\overline{)496}$

34) $6\overline{)791}$

35) $4\overline{)647}$

36) $7\overline{)780}$

37) $4\overline{)5910}$

38) $8\overline{)3515}$

39) $7\overline{)2355}$

40) $9\overline{)1232}$

41) $8\overline{)6029}$

42) $4\overline{)6743}$

Answers of Worksheets – Chapter 3

Multiplication

1) 228	7) 585	13) 16,252
2) 375	8) 320	14) 24,856
3) 532	9) 1,080	15) 30,498
4) 816	10) 2,252	16) 120
5) 572	11) 1,825	17) 60
6) 940	12) 2,225	

Division

1) 2	10) 7	19) 10
2) 12	11) 11	20) 132
3) 7	12) 12	21) 7
4) 15	13) 40	22) 8
5) 9	14) 10	23) 1
6) 21	15) 12	24) 12
7) 10	16) 10	25) 10
8) 4	17) 88	26) 9
9) 11	18) 132	27) 8

Long Division by One Digit

1) 5	15) 9	29) 34
2) 6	16) 9	30) 21
3) 6	17) 12	31) 23
4) 10	18) 12	32) 60
5) 7	19) 14	33) 16
6) 8	20) 16	34) 37
7) 5	21) 19	35) 14
8) 7	22) 21	36) 40
9) 7	23) 117	37) 144
10) 4	24) 45	38) 128
11) 9	25) 132	39) 142
12) 4	26) 70	40) 346
13) 9	27) 29	41) 204
14) 10	28) 13	42) 853

Division with Remainders

1) 5 *R*2	15) 9 *R*3	29) 146 *R*2
2) 9 *R*1	16) 9 *R*5	30) 96 *R*1
3) 4 *R*1	17) 21 *R*1	31) 53 *R*1
4) 3 *R*2	18) 13 *R*2	32) 410 *R*0
5) 5 *R*4	19) 14 *R*5	33) 99 *R*1
6) 8 *R*1	20) 24 *R*4	34) 131 *R*5
7) 5 *R*1	21) 23 *R*5	35) 161 *R*3
8) 4 *R*1	22) 36 *R*4	36) 111 *R*3
9) 8 *R*1	23) 66 *R*1	37) 1477 *R*2
10) 6 *R*4	24) 38 *R*4	38) 439 *R*3
11) 7 *R*3	25) 118 *R*4	39) 336 *R*3
12) 8 *R*3	26) 98 *R*1	40) 135 *R*8
13) 7 *R*2	27) 92 *R*1	41) 753 *R*5
14) 7 *R*1	28) 42 *R*4	42) 1,685 *R*3

Chapter 4: Mixed operations

Topics that you'll practice in this chapter:

- ✓ Rounding and Estimating
- ✓ Estimate Sums
- ✓ Estimate Differences
- ✓ Estimate Products
- ✓ Missing Numbers

Rounding and Estimating

✎ **Estimate the sum by rounding each number to the nearest ten.**

1) $14 + 68 =$

2) $82 + 12 =$

3) $43 + 66 =$

4) $47 + 65 =$

5) $553 + 232 =$

6) $418 + 846 =$

7) $582 + 277 =$

8) $2771 + 1651 =$

✎ **Estimate the product by rounding each number to the nearest ten.**

9) $55 \times 62 =$

10) $14 \times 27 =$

11) $34 \times 66 =$

12) $18 \times 12 =$

13) $62 \times 53 =$

14) $41 \times 26 =$

15) $19 \times 33 =$

16) $76 \times 45 =$

✎ **Estimate the sum or product by rounding each number to the nearest ten.**

17) $\begin{array}{r} 34 \\ \times\ 26 \\ \hline \end{array}$

18) $\begin{array}{r} 53 \\ \times\ 18 \\ \hline \end{array}$

19) $\begin{array}{r} 78 \\ +\ 92 \\ \hline \end{array}$

20) $\begin{array}{r} 55 \\ +9 \\ \hline \end{array}$

21) $\begin{array}{r} 73 \\ \times\ 12 \\ \hline \end{array}$

22) $\begin{array}{r} 81 \\ +\ 53 \\ \hline \end{array}$

Estimate Sums

✎ *Estimate the sum by rounding each added to the nearest ten.*

1) $55 + 9 =$

2) $13 + 74 =$

3) $83 + 7 =$

4) $32 + 37 =$

5) $13 + 74 =$

6) $34 + 11 =$

7) $39 + 77 =$

8) $25 + 4 =$

9) $61 + 73 =$

10) $64 + 59 =$

11) $14 + 68 =$

12) $82 + 12 =$

13) $43 + 66 =$

14) $45 + 65 =$

15) $96 + 94 =$

16) $29 + 89 =$

17) $78 + 74 =$

18) $39 + 27 =$

19) $91 + 68 =$

20) $48 + 81 =$

21) $14 + 96 =$

22) $52 + 59 =$

23) $553 + 232 =$

24) $52 + 67 =$

Estimate Differences

✎ *Estimate the difference by rounding each number to the nearest ten.*

1) $46 - 11 =$

2) $23 - 14 =$

3) $68 - 36 =$

4) $22 - 13 =$

5) $59 - 36 =$

6) $34 - 11 =$

7) $67 - 37 =$

8) $38 - 19 =$

9) $84 - 38 =$

10) $68 - 48 =$

11) $58 - 16 =$

12) $72 - 27 =$

13) $63 - 33 =$

14) $49 - 32 =$

15) $94 - 63 =$

16) $55 - 32 =$

17) $87 - 74 =$

18) $32 - 11 =$

19) $46 - 39 =$

20) $99 - 36 =$

21) $94 - 78 =$

22) $75 - 23 =$

23) $99 - 19 =$

24) $86 - 43 =$

Estimate Products

✍ *Estimate the products.*

1) $27 \times 18 =$

2) $13 \times 17 =$

3) $43 \times 19 =$

4) $22 \times 25 =$

5) $68 \times 23 =$

6) $36 \times 91 =$

7) $53 \times 92 =$

8) $18 \times 38 =$

9) $21 \times 14 =$

10) $83 \times 42 =$

11) $51 \times 32 =$

12) $68 \times 12 =$

13) $47 \times 23 =$

14) $71 \times 58 =$

15) $54 \times 89 =$

16) $37 \times 72 =$

17) $36 \times 93 =$

18) $32 \times 29 =$

19) $41 \times 37 =$

20) $54 \times 93 =$

21) $89 \times 72 =$

22) $77 \times 22 =$

23) $53 \times 13 =$

24) $98 \times 63 =$

Missing Numbers

✎ *Find the missing numbers.*

1) $20 \times \underline{} = 60$

2) $16 \times \underline{} = 32$

3) $\underline{} \times 14 = 84$

4) $16 \times \underline{} = 80$

5) $\underline{} \times 19 = 38$

6) $17 \times \underline{} = 34$

7) $\underline{} \times 1 = 18$

8) $21 \times \underline{} = 42$

9) $20 \times \underline{} = 80$

10) $15 \times 7 = \underline{}$

11) $18 \times 9 = \underline{}$

12) $21 \times 4 = \underline{}$

13) $23 \times 7 = \underline{}$

14) $\underline{} \times 25 = 75$

15) $24 \times \underline{} = 120$

16) $22 \times 4 = \underline{}$

17) $20 \times \underline{} = 140$

18) $17 \times \underline{} = 153$

19) $\underline{} \times 15 = 120$

20) $21 \times 6 = \underline{}$

21) $\underline{} \times 22 = 154$

22) $19 \times \underline{} = 76$

23) $23 \times 9 = \underline{}$

24) $25 \times 6 = \underline{}$

25) $\underline{} \times 18 = 36$

26) $24 \times \underline{} = 48$

Answers of Worksheets – Chapter 4

Rounding and Estimating

1) 80
2) 90
3) 110
4) 120
5) 780
6) 1,270
7) 860
8) 4,420

9) 3,600
10) 300
11) 2,100
12) 200
13) 3,000
14) 1,200
15) 600
16) 4,000

17) 900
18) 1,000
19) 170
20) 150
21) 700
22) 130

Estimate sums

1) 70
2) 80
3) 90
4) 70
5) 80
6) 40
7) 120
8) 30

9) 130
10) 120
11) 80
12) 90
13) 110
14) 120
15) 190
16) 120

17) 150
18) 70
19) 160
20) 130
21) 110
22) 110
23) 780
24) 120

Estimate differences

1) 40
2) 10
3) 30
4) 10
5) 20
6) 20
7) 30
8) 20

9) 40
10) 20
11) 40
12) 40
13) 30
14) 20
15) 30
16) 30

17) 20
18) 20
19) 10
20) 60
21) 10
22) 60
23) 80
24) 50

Estimate products

1) 600
2) 200
3) 600
4) 800
5) 1400
6) 3600

7) 4500
8) 800
9) 200
10) 3200
11) 1500
12) 700

13) 1000
14) 4200
15) 4500
16) 2800
17) 3600
18) 900

19) 1600	21) 6300	23) 500
20) 4500	22) 1600	24) 6000

Missing Numbers

1) 3	10) 105	19) 8
2) 2	11) 162	20) 126
3) 6	12) 84	21) 7
4) 5	13) 161	22) 4
5) 2	14) 3	23) 207
6) 2	15) 5	24) 150
7) 18	16) 88	25) 2
8) 2	17) 7	26) 2
9) 4	18) 9	

Chapter 5:
Algebra

Topics that you'll practice in this chapter:

- ✓ Evaluating Variable
- ✓ Evaluating Two Variables
- ✓ Solve Equations

Evaluating Variable

✍ *Simplify each algebraic expression.*

1) $5 + x$, $x = 2$

2) $x - 2$, $x = 4$

3) $8a + 1$, $a = 9$

4) $b - 12$, $b = -1$

5) $9 - x$, $x = 3$

6) $x + 2$, $x = 5$

7) $3m + 7$, $m = 6$

8) $a + (-5)$, $a = -2$

9) $3x + 6$, $x = 4$

10) $4q + 6$, $q = -1$

11) $10 + 2x - 6$, $x = 3$

12) $10 - 3x$, $x = 8$

13) $2x - 5$, $x = 4$

14) $5b + 6$, $b = -3$

15) $12x + 6$, $x = 2$

16) $10 - 3m$, $m = -2$

17) $5(6x + 2)$, $x = 8$

18) $2(-7b - 2)$, $b = 3$

19) $9x - 3x + 12$, $x = 6$

20) $(6a + 3) \div 5$, $a = 2$

21) $(x + 16) \div 3$, $x = 8$

22) $4x - 12 + 8x$, $x = -6$

23) $(16 - 12x)(-2)$, $x = -3$

24) $12p + 5p - 3$, $p = 2$

25) $x - 11x$, $x = -4$

26) $2a(6 - 4a)$, $a = 5$

27) $14y + 7 - 3y$, $y = -3$

28) $(-5)(10n - 20 + 2n)$, $n = 2$

29) $(-3) + \frac{x}{4} + 2x$, $x = 16$

30) $(-2) + \frac{x}{7}$, $x = 21$

31) $\left(-\frac{14}{x}\right) - 9 + 4x$, $x = 2$

32) $\left(-\frac{6}{x}\right) - 9 + 2x$, $x = 3$

Evaluating Two Variables

✏️ *Simplify each algebraic expression.*

1) $2x + 4y,$

   $x = 3, y = 2$

2) $8x + 5y,$

   $x = 1, y = 5$

3) $-2a + 4b,$

   $a = 6, b = 3$

4) $4x + 7 - 2y,$

   $x = 7, y = 6$

5) $5z + 12 - 4k,$

   $z = 5, k = 2$

6) $2(-x - 2y),$

   $x = 6, y = 9$

7) $18a + 2b,$

   $a = 2, b = 8$

8) $4x \div 3y,$

   $x = 3, y = 2$

9) $2x + 15 + 4y,$

   $x = -2, y = 4$

10) $4a - (15 - b),$

    $a = 4, b = 6$

11) $5z + 19 + 8k,$

    $z = -5, k = 4$

12) $xy + 12 + 5x,$

    $x = 7, y = 2$

13) $2x + 4y - 3 + 2,$

    $x = 5, y = 3$

14) $\left(-\frac{12}{x}\right) + 1 + 5y,$

    $x = 6, y = 8$

15) $(-4)(-2a - 2b),$

    $a = 5, b = 3$

16) $10 + 3x + 7 - 2y,$

    $x = 7, y = 6$

17) $9x + 2 - 4y + 5,$

    $x = 7, y = 5$

18) $6 + 3(-2x - 3y),$

    $x = 9, y = 7$

19) $2x + 14 + 4y,$

    $x = 6, y = 8$

20) $4a - (5a - b) + 5,$

    $a = 4, b = 6$

Solve Equations

✎*Solve each equation.*

1) $2x = 20, x =$ ____

2) $4x = 16, x =$ ____

3) $8x = 24, x =$ ____

4) $6x = 30, x =$ ____

5) $x + 5 = 8, x =$ ____

6) $x - 1 = 5, x =$ ____

7) $x - 8 = 3, x =$ ____

8) $x + 6 = 12, x =$ ____

9) $x - 2 = 17, x =$ ____

10) $8 = 12 + x, x =$ ____

11) $x - 5 = 4, x =$ ____

12) $2 - x = -12, x =$ ____

13) $16 = -4 + x, x =$ ____

14) $x - 4 = -25, x =$ ____

15) $x + 12 = -9, x =$ ____

16) $14 = 18 - x, x =$ ____

17) $2 + x = -14, x =$ ____

18) $x - 5 = 15, x =$ ____

19) $25 = x - 5, x =$ ____

20) $x - 3 = -12, x =$ ____

21) $x - 12 = 12, x =$ ____

22) $x - 12 = -25, x =$ ____

23) $x - 13 = 32, x =$ ____

24) $-55 = x - 18, x =$ ____

25) $x - 12 = 18, x =$ ____

26) $20 = 5x, x =$ ____

27) $x - 30 = 20, x =$ ____

28) $x - 12 = 32, x =$ ____

29) $36 - x = 3, x =$ ____

30) $x - 14 = 14, x =$ ____

31) $19 - x = -15, x =$ ____

32) $x - 19 = -35, x =$ ____

Answers of Worksheets – Chapter 5

Evaluating Variable

1) 7
2) 2
3) 73
4) −13
5) 6
6) 7
7) 25
8) −7
9) 18
10) 2
11) 10

12) −14
13) 3
14) −9
15) 30
16) 16
17) 250
18) −46
19) 48
20) 3
21) 8
22) −84

23) −104
24) 31
25) 40
26) −140
27) −26
28) −20
29) 33
30) 1
31) −8
32) −5

Evaluating Two Variables

1) 14
2) 33
3) 0
4) 23
5) 29
6) −48
7) 52
8) 2

9) 27
10) 7
11) 26
12) 61
13) 21
14) 39
15) 64

16) 26
17) 50
18) −111
19) 58
20) 7

Solve Equations

1) 10
2) 4
3) 3
4) 5
5) 3
6) 6
7) 11
8) 6
9) 19
10) −4
11) 9

12) 14
13) 20
14) −21
15) −21
16) 4
17) −16
18) 20
19) 30
20) −9
21) 24
22) −13

23) 45
24) −37
25) 30
26) 4
27) 50
28) 42
29) 33
30) 28
31) 34
32) −16

Chapter 6: Data and Graphs

Topics that you'll practice in this chapter:

- ✓ Graph Points on a Coordinate Plane
- ✓ Bar Graph
- ✓ Tally and Pictographs
- ✓ Line Graphs
- ✓ Stem–And–Leaf Plot
- ✓ Scatter Plots

Graph Points on a Coordinate Plane

✎ *Plot each point on the coordinate grid.*

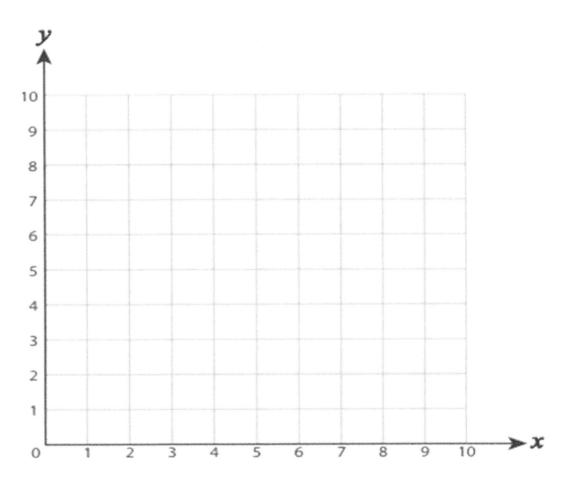

1) A (3, 6)

2) B (1, 3)

3) C (3, 7)

4) D (8, 6)

5) E (5, 2)

6) F (9, 3)

7) G (2, 1)

8) H (4, 2)

9) I (6, 6)

10) J (7, 2)

11) K (8, 3)

12) L (2, 9)

Bar Graph

✎ *Graph the given information as a bar graph.*

Day	Hot dogs sold
Monday	90
Tuesday	70
Wednesday	30
Thursday	20
Friday	60

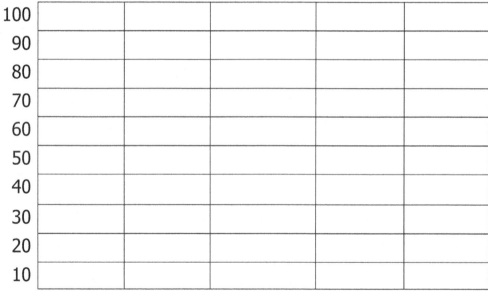

Tally and Pictographs

✎ *Using the key, draw the pictograph to show the information.*

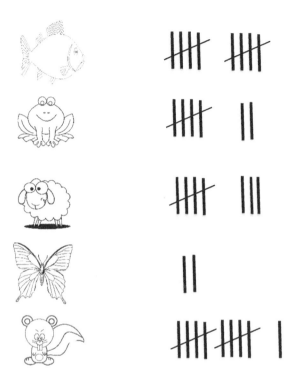

Key: 😊 = 2 animals

Line Graphs

David work as a salesman in a store. He records the number of shoes sold in five days on a line graph. Use the graph to answer the questions.

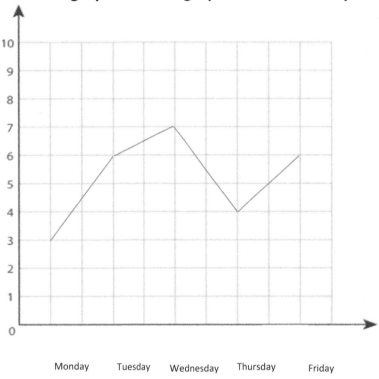

1) How many cars were sold on Monday?

2) Which day had the minimum sales of shoes?

3) Which day had the maximum number of shoes sold?

4) How many shoes were sold in 5 days?

Stem–And–Leaf Plot

Example:

56, 58, 42, 48, 66, 64, 53, 69, 45, 72

Stem	leaf		
4	2	5	8
5	3	6	8
6	4	6	9
7	2		

✎ *Make stem ad leaf plots for the given data.*

1) 74, 88, 97, 72, 79, 86, 95, 79, 83, 91

Stem | Leaf plot

2) 37, 48, 26, 33, 49, 26, 19, 26, 48

Stem | Leaf plot

3) 58, 41, 42, 67, 54, 65, 65, 54, 69, 53

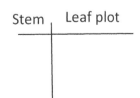

Stem | Leaf plot

Pie Graph

The circle graph below shows all Jason's expenses for last month. Jason spent $300 on his bills last month.

Answer following questions based on the Pie graph.

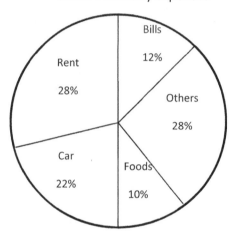

1- How much did Jason spend on his car last month? _____

2- How much did Jason spend for foods last month? _____

3- How much did Jason spend on his rent last month? _____

4- What fraction is Jason's expenses for his bills and Car out of his total

   expenses last month? _____

5- How much was Jason's total expenses last month? _____

Histograms

✍ *Use the following Graph to complete the table.*

Day	Distance (km)
1	
2	

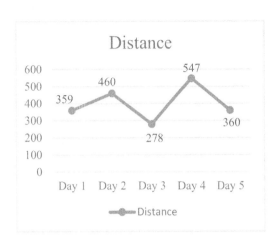

The following table shows the number of births in the US from 2007 to 2012 (in millions).

Year	Number of births (in millions)
2007	4.32
2008	4.25
2009	4.13
2010	4
2011	3.95
2012	3.95

Draw a histogram for the table.

Answers of Worksheets – Chapter 6

Graph Points on a Coordinate Plane

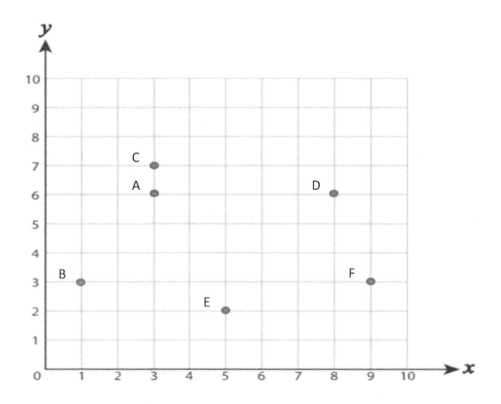

Bar Graph

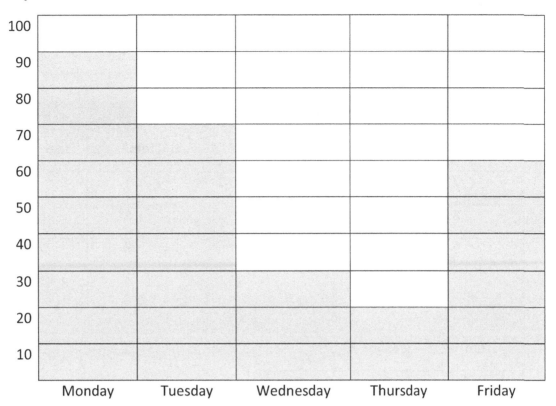

Tally and Pictographs

Line Graphs

1) 3
2) Thursday

3) Wednesday
4) 26

Stem–And–Leaf Plot

1)

Stem	leaf
7	2 4 9 9
8	3 6 8
9	1 5 7

2)

Stem	leaf
1	9
2	6 6 6
3	3 7
4	8 8 9

3)

Stem	leaf
4	1 2
5	3 4 4 8
6	5 5 7 9

Pie Graph

1) $550
2) $250
3) $700
4) $\frac{17}{50}$
5) $2,500

Histograms

Day	Distance (km)
1	359
2	460
3	278
4	547
5	360

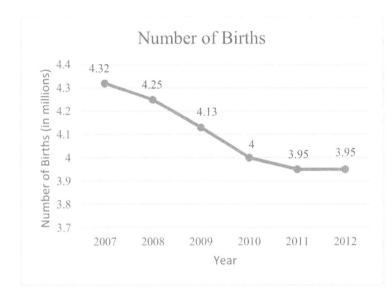

Chapter 7:
Patterns and Sequences

Topics that you'll practice in this chapter:

- ✓ Repeating pattern
- ✓ Growing Patterns
- ✓ Patterns: Numbers

Repeating Pattern

✎ *Circle the picture that comes next in each picture pattern.*

1)

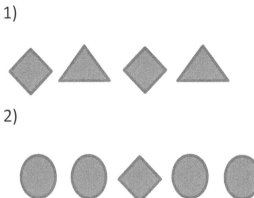 

2)

3)

4)

5)

6)

7)

Growing Patterns

✍ *Draw the picture that comes next in each growing pattern.*

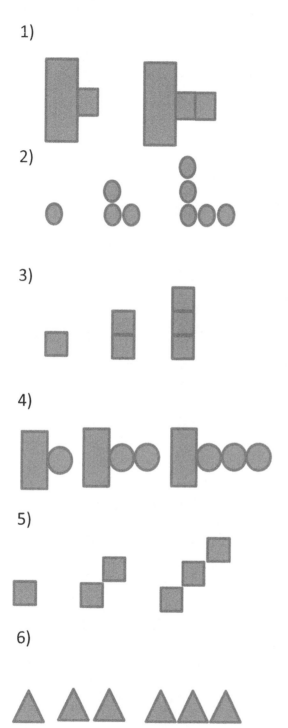

1)

2)

3)

4)

5)

6)

Patterns: Numbers

✍ **Write the numbers that come next.**

1) 12, 14, 16, 18,   _____, _____, _____, _____

2) 7, 14, 21, 28,   _____, _____, _____, _____

3) 15, 25, 35, 45,   _____, _____, _____, _____

4) 11, 22, 33, 44,   _____, _____, _____, _____

5) 10, 18, 26, 34, 42,   _____, _____, _____, _____

6) 61, 55, 49, 43, 37,   _____, _____, _____, _____

7) 45, 56, 67, 78,   _____, _____, _____, _____

✍ **Write the next three numbers in each counting sequence.**

8) −32, −23, −14, _____, _____, _____, _____

9) 543, 528, 513, _____, _____, _____, _____

10) _____, _____, 56, 64, _____, 80

11) 23, 34, _____, _____, 67, _____

12) 24, 31, _____, _____, _____

13) 52, 45, _____, _____, _____

14) 51, 44, 37, _____, _____, _____

15) 64, 51, 38, _____, _____, _____

Answers of Worksheets – Chapter 7

Repeating pattern

1)

2)

3)

4)

5)

6)

7)

Growing patterns

1)

2)

3)

4)

5)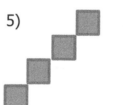

6)

Patterns: Numbers

1) $12, 14, 16, 18, 20, 22, 24, 26$
2) $7, 14, 21, 28, 35, 42, 49, 56$
3) $15, 25, 35, 45, 55, 65, 75, 85$
4) $11, 22, 33, 44, 55, 66, 77, 88$
5) $10, 18, 26, 34, 42, 50, 58, 66$
6) $61, 55, 49, 43, 37, 31, 25, 19$
7) $45, 56, 67, 78, 89, 100, 111, 122$
8) $-5, 4, 13, 22$
9) $498, 483, 468$
10) $40 - 48 - 56 - 64 - 72 - 80$
11) $23 - 34 - 45 - 56 - 67 - 78$
12) $38 - 45 - 52$
13) $38 - 31 - 24$
14) $30, 23, 16$
15) $25, 12, -1$

Chapter 8: Money

Topics that you'll practice in this chapter:

- ✓ Add Money Amounts
- ✓ Subtract Money Amounts
- ✓ Money: Word Problems

Adding Money Amounts

✎ *Add.*

1)
$$\begin{array}{r} \$314 \\ +\$152 \\ \hline \end{array}$$
$$\begin{array}{r} \$624 \\ +\$410 \\ \hline \end{array}$$
$$\begin{array}{r} \$390 \\ +\$215 \\ \hline \end{array}$$

2)
$$\begin{array}{r} \$321 \\ +\$430 \\ \hline \end{array}$$
$$\begin{array}{r} \$530 \\ +\$321 \\ \hline \end{array}$$
$$\begin{array}{r} \$712 \\ +\$145 \\ \hline \end{array}$$

3)
$$\begin{array}{r} \$411 \\ +\$316 \\ \hline \end{array}$$
$$\begin{array}{r} \$559 \\ +\$228 \\ \hline \end{array}$$
$$\begin{array}{r} \$731 \\ +\$213 \\ \hline \end{array}$$

4)
$$\begin{array}{r} \$621 \\ +\$168 \\ \hline \end{array}$$
$$\begin{array}{r} \$321 \\ +\$129 \\ \hline \end{array}$$
$$\begin{array}{r} \$615 \\ +\$371 \\ \hline \end{array}$$

5)
$$\begin{array}{r} \$526 \\ +\$228 \\ \hline \end{array}$$
$$\begin{array}{r} \$287 \\ +\$129 \\ \hline \end{array}$$
$$\begin{array}{r} \$493 \\ +\$274 \\ \hline \end{array}$$

6)
$$\begin{array}{r} \$386 \\ +\$464 \\ \hline \end{array}$$
$$\begin{array}{r} \$275 \\ +\$175 \\ \hline \end{array}$$
$$\begin{array}{r} \$636 \\ +\$295 \\ \hline \end{array}$$

7)
$$\begin{array}{r} \$489 \\ +\ \$378 \\ \hline \end{array}$$
$$\begin{array}{r} \$579 \\ +\$459 \\ \hline \end{array}$$
$$\begin{array}{r} \$737 \\ +\$462 \\ \hline \end{array}$$

Subtracting Money Amounts

✎ *Subtract.*

1)
$825
−$166
—————

$651
−$110
—————

$754
−$565
—————

2)
$539
−$137
—————

$498
−$359
—————

$992
−$549
—————

3)
$436
−$219
—————

$512
−$128
—————

$632
−$444
—————

4)
$345
−$127
—————

$419
−$361
—————

$397
−$231
—————

5)
$452
−$298
—————

$583
−$362
—————

$684
−$495
—————

6)
$735
−$599
—————

$829
−$714
—————

$984
−$582
—————

7) Linda had $12.00. She bought some game tickets for $7.14. How much did she have left?

Money: Word Problems

✎ *Solve each word problem.*

1) How many boxes of envelopes can you buy with $18 if one box costs $3?_____

2) After paying $6.25 for a salad, Ella has $45.56. How much money did she have before buying the salad? _____

3) How many packages of diapers can you buy with $50 if one package costs $5? _____

4) Last week James ran 20 miles more than Michael. James ran 56 miles. How many miles did Michael run? _____

5) Last Friday Jacob had $32.52. Over the weekend he received some money for cleaning the attic. He now has $44. How much money did he receive? _____

6) After paying $10.12 for a sandwich, Amelia has $35.50. How much money did she have before buying the sandwich? _____

7) How many packages of pencils can you buy with $42.00 if one package costs $3.50? _____

8) At the mall Todd purchased 13 video games which cost $6.27 each. If he had $100 in his wallet before the purchase, how much money is left in his wallet? _____

9) 8.4 pounds of apples costs $10.08. What is the price per pound? _____

10) Daniel earns $13.50 per hour working as a bank clerk. If he works 44 hours a week, how much does he earn per week? _____

Answers of Worksheets – Chapter 8

Add Money Amounts

1) $466, 1,034, 605$
2) $751, 851, 857$
3) $727, 787, 944$
4) $789, 450, 986$
5) $754, 416, 767$
6) $850, 450, 931$
7) $867, 1,038, 1,199$

Subtract Money Amounts

1) $659 – 541 – 189$
2) $402 – 139 – 443$
3) $217 – 384 – 188$
4) $218, 58, 166$
5) $154, 221, 189$
6) $136, 115, 402$
7) 4.86

Money: word problem

1) 6
2) $51.81
3) 10
4) 36
5) 11.48
6) 45.62
7) 12
8) $18.49
9) $1.20
10) $594

Chapter 9: Measurements

Topics that you'll practice in this chapter:

- ✓ Convert Measurement Units
- ✓ Metric units
- ✓ Distance Measurement
- ✓ Weight Measurement

Convert Measurement Units

✍ **Convert to an appropriate measurement unit. (Round to the nearest Hundredths)**

1) 4 m = _____ cm

2) 50 cm = _____ m

3) 5 m = _____ cm

4) 3 feet = _____ inches

5) 5 feet = _____ cm

6) 2 feet = _____ inches

7) 1 inch = _____ cm

8) 4 feet = _____ inches

9) 8 inches = _____ foot

10) 10 feet = _____ m

11) 15 cm = _____ m

12) 5 inches = _____ cm

13) 10 inches = _____ m

14) 15 inches = _____ cm

15) 12 inches = _____ m

16) 8 feet = _____ inches

17) 25 cm = _____ inches

18) 11 inches = _____ cm

19) 1 m = _____ inches

20) 80 inches = _____ m

21) 200 cm = _____ m

22) 5 m = _____ cm

23) 12 feet = _____ inches

24) 10 yards = _____ inches

25) 16 feet = _____ inches

26) 48 inches = _____ Feet

27) 4 inches = _____ cm

28) 12.5 cm = _____ inches

29) 6 feet = _____ inches

30) 10 feet = _____ inches

31) 12 yards = _____ feet

32) 7 yards = _____ feet

Metric Units

✍ *Convert to an appropriate Metric unit.*

1) 1 cm = _____ mm

2) 1 m = _____ mm

3) 5 cm = _____ mm

4) 0.1 cm = _____ mm

5) 0.2 m = _____ cm

6) 10 mm = _____ cm

7) 50 mm = _____ m

8) 10 cm = _____ m

9) 100 mm = _____ cm

10) 0.05 m = _____ mm

11) 1 km = _____ m

12) 0.01 km = _____ m

13) 500 cm = _____ m

14) 0.50 km _____ m

15) 100 cm = _____ m

16) 80 cm = _____ mm

17) 4 mm = _____ cm

18) 0.6 m = _____ mm

19) 2 m = _____ cm

20) 0.03 km = _____ m

21) 3000 mm = _____ km

22) 5 cm = _____ m

23) 0.03 m = _____ cm

24) 1000 mm = _____ km

25) 600 mm = _____ m

26) 0.77 km = _____ mm

27) 0.08 km = _____ m

28) 0.30 m = _____ cm

29) 400 m = _____ km

30) 5000 cm = _____ km

31) 40 mm = _____ cm

32) 800 m = _____ km

Distance Measurement

✍ *Convert to the new units. (Round to the nearest Hundredths)*

1) 1 mi = _____ ft

2) 1 mi = _____ yd

3) 1 yd = _____ m

4) 2 yd = _____ ft

5) 2 mi = _____ yd

6) 3 mi = _____ m

7) 5 mi = _____ ft

8) 6 m = _____ ft

9) 4 mi = _____ m

10) 10 mi = _____ yd

11) 9 mi = _____ yd

12) 12 mi = _____ yd

13) 10 mi = _____ ft

14) 15 mi = _____ ft

15) 20 mi = _____ yd

16) 16 mi = _____ yd

17) 2 mi = _____ ft

18) 21 mi = _____ ft

19) 6 mi = _____ ft

20) 3 mi = _____ yd

21) 72 mi = _____ ft

22) 41 mi = _____ yd

23) 62 mi = _____ yd

24) 39 mi = _____ yd

25) 7 mi = _____ yd

26) 94 mi = _____ yd

27) 87 mi = _____ yd

28) 23 mi = _____ yd

29) 2 mi = _____ m

30) 5 mi = _____ m

31) 6 mi = _____ m

32) 3 mi = _____ m

Weight Measurement

✍ *Convert to grams.*

1) 1 kg = _____ g

2) 3 kg = _____ g

3) 5 kg = _____ g

4) 4 kg = _____ g

5) 0.01 kg = _____ g

6) 0.2 kg = _____ g

7) 0.04 kg = _____ g

8) 0.05 kg = _____ g

9) 0.5 kg = _____ g

10) 3.2 kg = _____ g

11) 8.2 kg = _____ g

12) 9.2 kg = _____ g

13) 35 kg = _____ g

14) 87 kg = _____ g

15) 45 kg = _____ g

16) 15 kg = _____ g

17) 0.32 kg = _____ g

18) 81 kg = _____ g

✍ *Convert to kilograms.*

19) 10,000 g = _____ kg

20) 20,000 g = _____ kg

21) 3,000 g = _____ kg

22) 100,000 g = _____ kg

23) 150,000 g = _____ kg

24) 120,000 g = _____ kg

25) 200,000 g = _____ kg

26) 30,000 g = _____ kg

27) 800,000 g = _____ kg

28) 20,000 g = _____ kg

29) 40,000 g = _____ kg

30) 500,000 g = _____ kg

Answers of Worksheets – Chapter 9

Inches & Centimeters

1) 4 m = 400 cm
2) 50 cm = 0.5 m
3) 5 m = 500 cm
4) 3 feet = 36 inches
5) 5 feet = 152.4 cm
6) 2 feet = 24 inches
7) 1 inch = 2.54 cm
8) 4 feet = 48 inches
9) 8 inches = 0.67 foot
10) 10 feet = 3.05 m
11) 15 cm = 0.15 m
12) 5 inches = 12.7 cm
13) 10 inches = 0.25 m
14) 15 inches = 38.1 cm
15) 12 inches = 0.3 m
16) 8 feet = 96 inches

17) 25 cm = 9.84 inches
18) 11 inch = 27.94 cm
19) 1 m = 39.37 inches
20) 80 inch = 2.03 m
21) 200 cm = 2 m
22) 5 m = 500 cm
23) 12 feet = 144 inches
24) 10 yards = 360 inches
25) 16 feet = 192 inches
26) 48 inches = 4 Feet
27) 4 inch = 10.16 cm
28) 12.5 cm = 4.92 inches
29) 6 feet = 72 inches
30) 10 feet = 120 inches
31) 12 yards = 36 feet
32) 7 yards = 21 feet

Metric Units

1) 1 cm = 10 mm
2) 1 m = 1000 mm
3) 5 cm = 50 mm
4) 0.1 cm = 1 mm
5) 0.2 m = 20 cm
6) 10 mm = 1 cm
7) 50 mm = 0.05 m
8) 10 cm = 0.10 m
9) 100 mm = 10 cm
10) 0.05 m = 50 mm
11) 1 km = 1,000 m
12) 0.01 km = 10 m
13) 500 cm = 5 m
14) 0.50 km = 500 m
15) 100 cm = 1 m
16) 80 cm = 800 mm

17) 4 mm = 0.4 cm
18) 0.6 m = 600 mm
19) 2 m = 200 cm
20) 0.03 km = 30 m
21) 3,000 mm = 0.003 km
22) 5 cm = 0.05 m
23) 0.03 m = 3 cm
24) 1,000 mm = 0.001 km
25) 600 mm = 0.6 m
26) 0.77 km = 770,000 mm
27) 0.08 km = 80 m
28) 0.30 m = 30 cm
29) 400 m = 0.4 km
30) 5,000 cm = 0.05 km
31) 40 mm = 4 cm
32) 800 m = 0.8 km

Distance Measurement

1) 1 mi = 5,280 ft
2) 1 mi = 1,760 yd
3) 1 yd = 0.91 m
4) 2 yd = 6 ft
5) 2 mi = 3,520 yd
6) 3 mi = 4,828 m
7) 5 mi = 26,400 ft
8) 6 m = 20 ft
9) 4 mi = 6,437 m
10) 10 mi = 17,600 yd
11) 9 mi = 15,840 yd
12) 12 mi = 21,120 yd
13) 10 mi = 52,800 ft
14) 15 mi = 79,200 ft
15) 20 mi = 35,200 yd
16) 16 mi = 28,160 yd

17) 21 mi = 110,880 ft
18) 6 mi = 31,680 ft
19) 3 mi = 5,280 yd
20) 72 mi = 380,160 ft
21) 41 mi = 72,160 yd
22) 62 mi = 109,120 yd
23) 39 mi = 68,640 yd
24) 7 mi = 12,320 yd
25) 94 mi = 165,440 yd
26) 87 mi = 153,120 yd
27) 23 mi = 40,480 yd
28) 2 mi = 3,219 m
29) 5 mi = 8,047 m
30) 6 mi = 9,656 m
31) 3 mi = 4828 m

Weight Measurement

1) 1 kg = 1,000 g
2) 3 kg = 3,000 g
3) 5 kg = 5,000 g
4) 4 kg = 4,000 g
5) 0.01 kg = 10 g
6) 0.2 kg = 200 g
7) 0.04 kg = 40 g
8) 0.05 kg = 50 g
9) 0.5 kg = 500 g
10) 3.2 kg = 3,200 g
11) 8.2 kg = 8,200 g
12) 9.2 kg = 9,200 g
13) 35 kg = 35,000 g
14) 87 kg = 87,000 g
15) 45 kg = 45,000 g

16) 15 kg = 15,000 g
17) 0.32 kg = 320 g
18) 81 kg = 81,000 g
19) 10,000 g = 10 kg
20) 20,000 g = 20 kg
21) 3,000 g = 3 kg
22) 100,000 g = 100 kg
23) 150,000 g = 150 kg
24) 120,000 g = 120 kg
25) 200,000 g = 200 kg
26) 30,000 g = 30 kg
27) 800,000 g = 800 kg
28) 20,000 g = 20 kg
29) 40,000 g = 40 kg
30) 500,000 g = 500 kg

Chapter 10: Time

Topics that you'll practice in this chapter:

- ✓ Read Clocks
- ✓ Telling Time
- ✓ Digital Clock
- ✓ Measurement – Time

Read Clocks

✎ *Write the time below each clock.*

1) _____

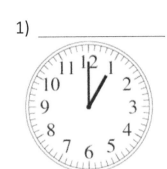

2) _____

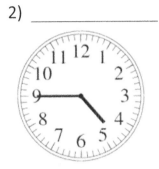

3) _____

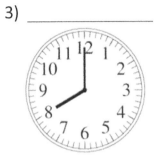

4) _____

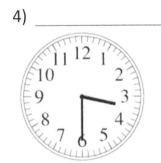

5) _____

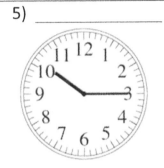

6) _____

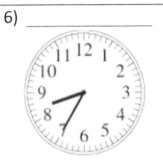

✎ *How much time has passed?*

7) From 1:15 AM to 4:35 AM: _____ hours and _____ minutes.

8) From 1:25 AM to 4:05 AM: _____ hours and _____ minutes.

9) It's 8:30 P.M. What time was 5 hours ago?

_____ O'clock

Digital Clock

✍ *What time is it? Write the time in words in front of each.*

1) 2 : 30   _____

2) 3 : 15   _____

3) 5 : 45   _____

4) 9 : 20   _____

5) 10 : 5   _____

6) 12 : 50   _____

7) 10 : 25   _____

8) 3 : 23   _____

9) 11 : 57   _____

10) 2 : 12   _____

11) 1 : 02   _____

12) 8 : 35   _____

Measurement – Time

✎ How much time has passed?

1) 1:15 AM to 4:35 AM: _____ hours and _____ minutes.

2) 2:35 AM to 5:10 AM: _____ hours and _____ minutes.

3) 6:00 AM. to 7:25 AM. = _____ hour(s) and _____ minutes.

4) 6:15 PM to 7:30 PM. = _____ hour(s) and _____ minutes

5) 5:15 A.M. to 5:45 A.M. = _____ minutes

6) 4:05 A.M. to 4:30 A.M. = _____ minutes

7) There are _____ second in 15 minutes.

8) There are _____ second in 11 minutes.

9) There are _____ second in 27 minutes.

10) There are _____ minutes in 10 hours.

11) There are _____ minutes in 20 hours.

12) There are _____ minutes in 12 hours.

Answers of Worksheets – Chapter 10

Read clocks

1) 1
2) 4 : 45
3) 8
4) 3 : 30
5) 10 : 15
6) 8 : 35
7) 3 hours and 20 minutes
8) 2 hours and 40 minutes
9) 3 : 30 PM

Digital Clock

1) It's two thirty.
2) It's three Fifteen.
3) It's five forty–five.
4) It's nine twenty.
5) It's ten five.
6) It's Twelve Fifty.
7) It's ten Twenty–five.
8) It's three Twenty–three.
9) It's Eleven fifty seven.
10) It's two Twelve.
11) It's one two.
12) It's eight thirty five.

Measurement – Time

1) 3 : 20
2) 2 : 35
3) 1 : 25
4) 1 : 15
5) 30 minutes
6) 25 minutes
7) 900
8) 660
9) 1,620
10) 600
11) 1,200
12) 720

Chapter 11: Geometry

Topics that you'll practice in this chapter:

- ✓ Identifying Angles: Acute, Right, Obtuse, and Straight Angles
- ✓ Polygon Names
- ✓ Classify Triangles
- ✓ Parallel Sides in Quadrilaterals
- ✓ Identify Rectangles
- ✓ Perimeter: Find the Missing Side Lengths
- ✓ Perimeter and Area of Squares
- ✓ Perimeter and Area of rectangles
- ✓ Area of Rectangles
- ✓ Area and Perimeter: Word Problems
- ✓ Area of Squares and Rectangles
- ✓ Volume of Cubes and Rectangle Prisms

Identifying Angles: Acute, Right, Obtuse, and Straight Angles

✍ *Write the name of the angles.*

1)

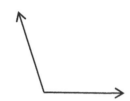

2)

3)

4)

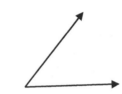

5)

6)

7)

8)

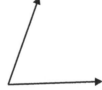

Polygon Names

✎ *Write name of polygons.*

1)

2)

3)

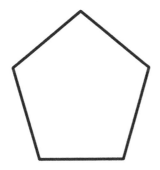

4)

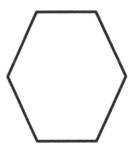

5)

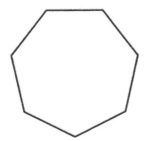

6)

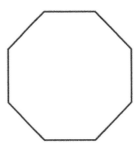

7)

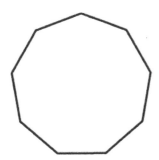

8)

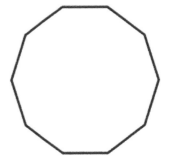

Triangles

✍ *Classify the triangles by their sides and angles.*

1)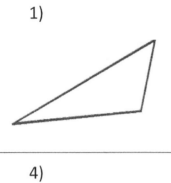

2)

3)

4)

5)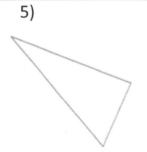

6)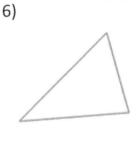

✍ *Find the measure of the unknown angle in each triangle.*

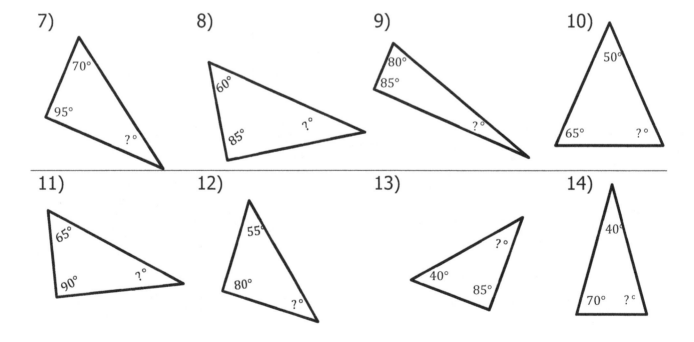

7) 70° 95° ?°

8) 60° 85° ?°

9) 80° 85° ?°

10) 50° 65° ?°

11) 65° 90° ?°

12) 55° 80° ?°

13) ?° 40° 85°

14) 40° 70° ?°

Quadrilaterals and Rectangles

✎ *Write the appropriate name of each quadrilateral.*

1)

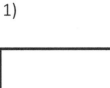

2)

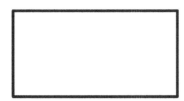

3)

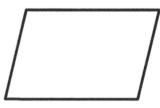

4)

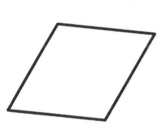

5)

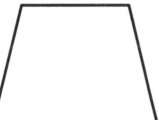

6)

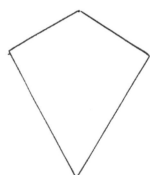

✎ **Solve.**

7) A rectangle has _____ sides and _____ angles.

8) Draw a rectangle that is 6 centimeters long and 3 centimeters wide. What is the perimeter?

9) Draw a rectangle 5 cm long and 2 cm wide.

10) Draw a rectangle whose length is 4 cm and whose width is 2 cm. What is the perimeter of the rectangle?

11) What is the perimeter of the rectangle?

8

4

Perimeter: Find the Missing Side Lengths

✍ *Find the missing side of each shape.*

1) perimeter = 44

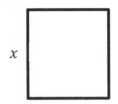

2) perimeter = 28

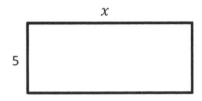

3) perimeter = 30

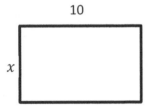

4) perimeter = 16

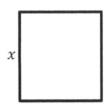

5) perimeter = 60

6) perimeter = 22

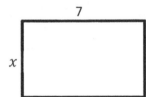

7) perimeter = 30

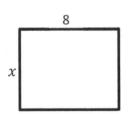

8) perimeter = 36

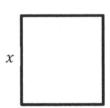

9) perimeter = 50

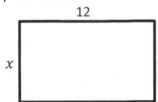

10) perimeter = 48

Perimeter and Area of Squares

 *Find perimeter and area of squares.*

1) A: _____ , P: _____

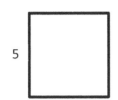

5

2) A: _____ , P: _____

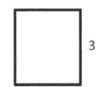

3

3) A: _____ , P: _____

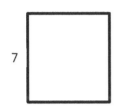

7

4) A: _____ , P: _____

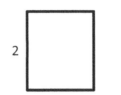

2

5) A: _____ , P: _____

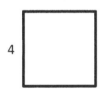

4

6) A: _____ , P: _____

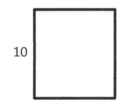

10

7) A: _____ , P: _____

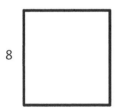

8

8) A: _____ , P: _____

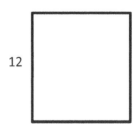

12

9) A: _____ , P: _____

15

10) A: _____ , P: _____

18

Perimeter and Area of rectangles

✍ *Find perimeter and area of rectangles.*

1) A: _____ , P: _____

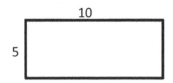

10

5

2) A: _____ , P: _____

6

4

3) A: _____ , P: _____

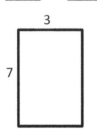

3

7

4) A: _____ , P: _____

15

10

5) A: _____ , P: _____

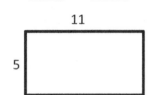

11

5

6) A: _____ , P: _____

9

8

7) A: _____ , P: _____

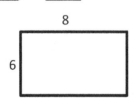

8

6

8) A: _____ , P: _____

15

6

9) A: _____ , P: _____

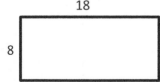

18

8

10) A: _____ , P: _____

20

10

Area of Rectangles

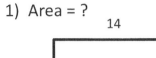 *Find area or missing side length of rectangles.*

1) Area = ?

14

5

2) Area = 48, x = ?

8

x

3) Area = 40, x = ?

4

x

4) Area = ?

12

8

5) Area = ?

22

15

6) Area = 600, x = ?

20

x

7) Area = 384, x = ?

32

x

8) Area = 525, x = ?

x

21

9) Area = 450, x = ?

30

x

10) Area = 990, x = ?

55

x

Area and Perimeter

✎ *Find the area of each.*

1)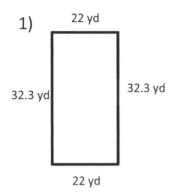

2)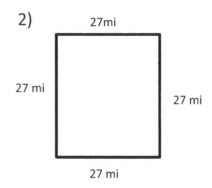

✎ **Solve.**

3) The area of a rectangle is 72 square meters. The width is 8 meters. What is the length of the rectangle?

4) A square has an area of 36 square feet. What is the perimeter of the square?

5) Ava built a rectangular vegetable garden that is 6 feet long and has an area of 54 square feet. What is the perimeter of Ava's vegetable garden?

6) A square has a perimeter of 64 millimeters. What is the area of the square?

7) The perimeter of David's square backyard is 44 meters. What is the area of David's backyard?

8) The area of a rectangle is 40 square inches. The length is 8 inches. What is the perimeter of the rectangle?

Volume of Cubes

✐ *Find the volume of each cube.*

1)

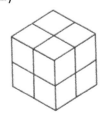

2)

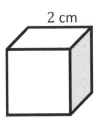

3)

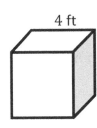

4)

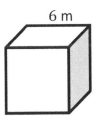

5)

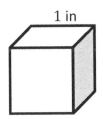

6)

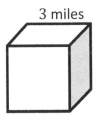

7)

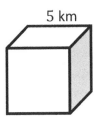

8)

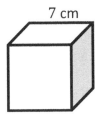

9)

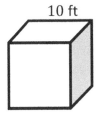

10)

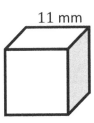

11)

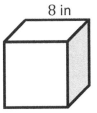

12)

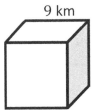

Answers of Worksheets – Chapter 11

Identifying Angles: Acute, Right, Obtuse, and Straight Angles

1) Obtuse
2) Acute
3) Right
4) Acute
5) Straight
6) Obtuse
7) Obtuse
8) Acute

Polygon Names

1) Triangle
2) Quadrilateral
3) Pentagon
4) Hexagon
5) Heptagon
6) Octagon
7) Nonagon
8) Decagon

Triangles

1) Scalene, obtuse
2) Isosceles, right
3) Scalene, right
4) Equilateral, acute
5) Scalene, acute
6) Scalene, acute
7) $15°$
8) $35°$
9) $15°$
10) $65°$
11) $25°$
12) $45°$
13) $55°$
14) $70°$

Quadrilaterals and Rectangles

1) Square
2) Rectangle
3) Parallelogram
4) Rhombus
5) Trapezoid
6) Kike
7) $4 - 4$
8) 18
9) Use a rule to draw the rectangle
10) 12
11) 24

Perimeter: Find the Missing Side Lengths

1) 11
2) 9
3) 5
4) 4
5) 15
6) 4
7) 7
8) 9
9) 13
10) 18

Perimeter and Area of Squares

1) $A: 25, P: 20$
2) $A: 9, P: 12$
3) $A: 49, P: 28$
4) $A: 4, P: 8$
5) $A: 16, P: 16$
6) $A: 100, P: 40$
7) $A: 64, P: 32$
8) $A: 144, P: 48$
9) $A: 225, P: 60$
10) $A: 324, P: 72$

Perimeter and Area of rectangles

1) $A: 50, P: 30$
2) $A: 24, P: 20$
3) $A: 21, P: 20$
4) $A: 150, P: 50$

5) $A: 55, P: 32$
6) $A: 72, P: 34$
7) $A: 48, P: 28$
8) $A: 90, P: 42$

9) $A: 144, P: 52$
10) $A: 200, P: 60$

Find the Area or Missing Side Length of a Rectangle

1) 70
2) 6
3) 10
4) 96
5) 330

6) 30
7) 12
8) 25
9) 15
10) 18

Area and Perimeter

1) $710.6 \ yd^2$
2) $729 \ mi^2$
3) 9

4) 24
5) 30
6) 256
7) 121
8) 26

Volume of Cubes

1) $50.24 \ in^2$
2) $113.04 \ cm^2$
3) $12.56 \ ft^2$
4) $314 \ m^2$
5) $28.26 \ cm^2$
6) $200.96 \ miles^2$

7) $12.56 \ in^2$
8) $3.14 \ ft^2$
9) $50.24 \ m^2$
10) $78.5 \ cm^2$
11) $113.04 \ miles^2$
12) $19.63 \ ft^2$

Chapter 12: Three-Dimensional Figures

Topics that you'll practice in this chapter:

- ✓ Identify Three–Dimensional Figures
- ✓ Count Vertices, Edges, and Faces
- ✓ Identify Faces of Three–Dimensional Figures

Identify Three–Dimensional Figures

✍ *Write the name of each shape.*

1)

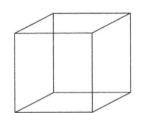

2)

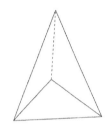

3)

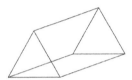

4)

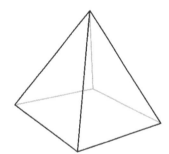

5)

6)

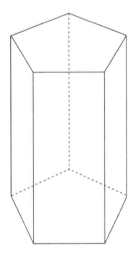

7)

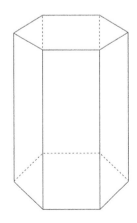

Count Vertices, Edges, and Faces

	Number of edges	Number of faces	Number of vertices

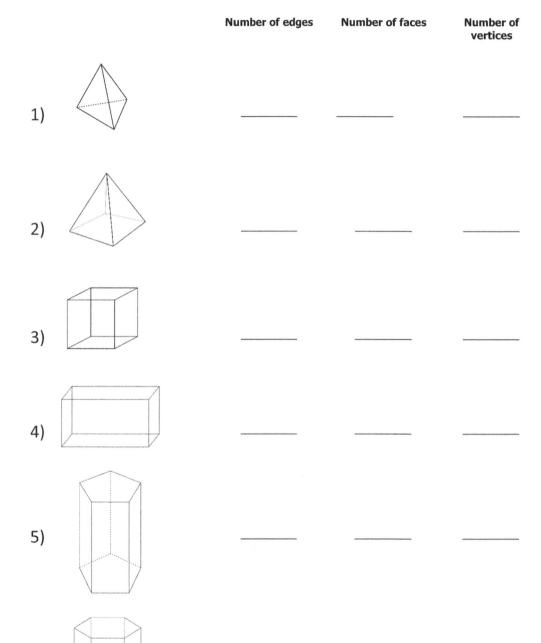

1) _____   _____   _____

2) _____   _____   _____

3) _____   _____   _____

4) _____   _____   _____

5) _____   _____   _____

6) _____   _____   _____

Identify Faces of Three–Dimensional Figures

✎ *Write the number of faces.*

1)

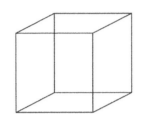

2)

3)

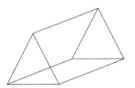

4)

5)

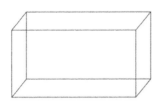

6)

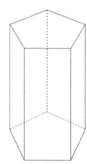

7)

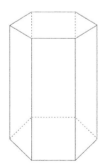

8)

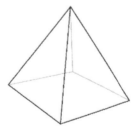

Answers of Worksheets – Chapter 12

Identify Three–Dimensional Figures

1) Cube
2) Triangular pyramid
3) Triangular prism
4) Square pyramid

5) Rectangular prism
6) Pentagonal prism
7) Hexagonal prism

Count Vertices, Edges, and Faces

	Number of edges	Number of faces	Number of vertices
1)	6	4	4
2)	8	5	5
3)	12	6	8
4)	12	6	8

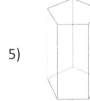

5)   15   7   10

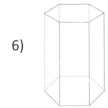

6)   18   8   12

Identify Faces of Three–Dimensional Figures

1) 6
2) 2
3) 5
4) 4
5) 6
6) 7
7) 8
8) 5

Chapter 13: Symmetry and Transformations

Topics that you'll practice in this chapter:

- ✓ Line Segments
- ✓ Identify Lines of Symmetry
- ✓ Count Lines of Symmetry
- ✓ Parallel, Perpendicular and Intersecting Lines

Line Segments

✍ *Write each as a line, ray or line segment.*

1)

2)

3)

4)

5)

6)

7)

8)

Identify Lines of Symmetry

✍ *Tell whether the line on each shape is a line of symmetry.*

1)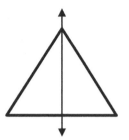

2)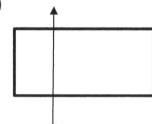

3)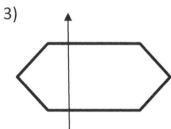

4)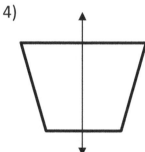

5)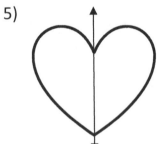

6)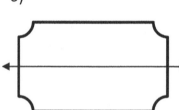

7)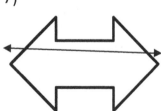

8)

Count Lines of Symmetry

✎ *Draw lines of symmetry on each shape. Count and write the lines of symmetry you see.*

1)

2)
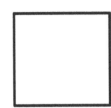

3)

4)

5)

6)

7)
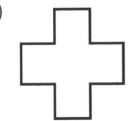

8)

Parallel, Perpendicular and Intersecting Lines

✍ *State whether the given pair of lines are parallel, perpendicular, or intersecting.*

1)

2)

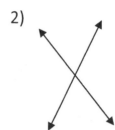

3)

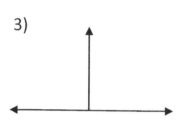

4)

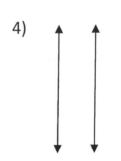

5)

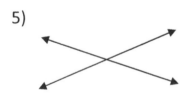

6)

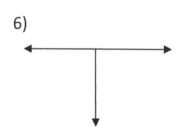

7)

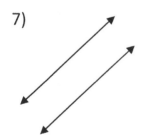

8)

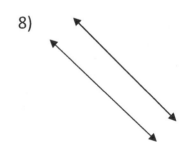

Answers of Worksheets – Chapter 13

Line Segments

1) Line segment
2) Ray
3) Line
4) Line segment

5) Ray
6) Line
7) Line
8) Line segment

Identify lines of symmetry

1) yes
2) no
3) no

4) yes
5) yes
6) yes

7) no
8) yes

Count lines of symmetry

1)

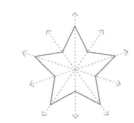

2)

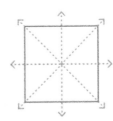

3)

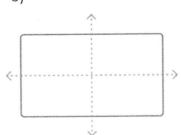

4)

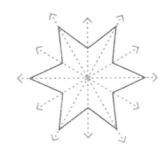

5)

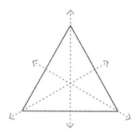

6)

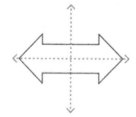

7)

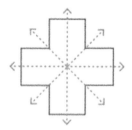

8)

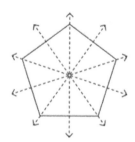

Parallel, Perpendicular and Intersecting Lines

1) Parallel

2) Intersection

3) Perpendicular

4) Parallel

5) Intersection

6) Perpendicular

7) Parallel

8) Parallel

Chapter 14:
Fractions

Topics that you'll practice in this chapter:

- ✓ Fractions

- ✓ Add Fractions with Like Denominators

- ✓ Subtract Fractions with Like Denominators

- ✓ Add and Subtract Fractions with Like Denominators

- ✓ Compare Sums and Differences of Fractions with Like Denominators

- ✓ Add 3 or More Fractions with Like Denominators

- ✓ Simplifying Fractions

- ✓ Add Fractions with Unlike Denominators

- ✓ Subtract Fractions with Unlike Denominators

- ✓ Add Fractions with Denominators of 10 and 100

- ✓ Add and Subtract Fractions with Denominators of 10, 100, and 1000

Add Fractions with Like Denominators

✎ *Add fractions.*

1) $\dfrac{2}{3} + \dfrac{1}{3} =$

2) $\dfrac{3}{5} + \dfrac{2}{5} =$

3) $\dfrac{5}{8} + \dfrac{4}{8} =$

4) $\dfrac{3}{4} + \dfrac{3}{4} =$

5) $\dfrac{4}{10} + \dfrac{3}{10} =$

6) $\dfrac{3}{7} + \dfrac{2}{7} =$

7) $\dfrac{4}{5} + \dfrac{4}{5} =$

8) $\dfrac{5}{14} + \dfrac{7}{14} =$

9) $\dfrac{5}{18} + \dfrac{11}{18} =$

10) $\dfrac{3}{12} + \dfrac{5}{12} =$

11) $\dfrac{5}{13} + \dfrac{5}{13} =$

12) $\dfrac{8}{25} + \dfrac{12}{25} =$

13) $\dfrac{9}{15} + \dfrac{6}{15} =$

14) $\dfrac{4}{20} + \dfrac{5}{20} =$

15) $\dfrac{9}{17} + \dfrac{3}{17} =$

16) $\dfrac{18}{32} + \dfrac{15}{32} =$

17) $\dfrac{12}{28} + \dfrac{10}{28} =$

18) $\dfrac{4}{20} + \dfrac{8}{20} =$

19) $\dfrac{24}{45} + \dfrac{11}{45} =$

20) $\dfrac{8}{36} + \dfrac{18}{36} =$

21) $\dfrac{19}{30} + \dfrac{12}{30} =$

22) $\dfrac{23}{42} + \dfrac{10}{42} =$

Subtract Fractions with Like Denominators

✍ *Subtract fractions.*

1) $\dfrac{4}{5} - \dfrac{2}{5} =$

2) $\dfrac{2}{3} - \dfrac{1}{3} =$

3) $\dfrac{7}{9} - \dfrac{4}{9} =$

4) $\dfrac{5}{6} - \dfrac{3}{6} =$

5) $\dfrac{4}{10} - \dfrac{3}{10} =$

6) $\dfrac{5}{7} - \dfrac{3}{7} =$

7) $\dfrac{7}{8} - \dfrac{5}{8} =$

8) $\dfrac{11}{13} - \dfrac{9}{13} =$

9) $\dfrac{8}{10} - \dfrac{5}{10} =$

10) $\dfrac{8}{12} - \dfrac{7}{12} =$

11) $\dfrac{18}{21} - \dfrac{12}{21} =$

12) $\dfrac{15}{19} - \dfrac{9}{19} =$

13) $\dfrac{9}{25} - \dfrac{6}{25} =$

14) $\dfrac{25}{32} - \dfrac{17}{32} =$

15) $\dfrac{22}{27} - \dfrac{9}{27} =$

16) $\dfrac{27}{30} - \dfrac{15}{30} =$

17) $\dfrac{31}{33} - \dfrac{26}{33} =$

18) $\dfrac{18}{28} - \dfrac{8}{28} =$

19) $\dfrac{35}{40} - \dfrac{15}{40} =$

20) $\dfrac{29}{35} - \dfrac{19}{35} =$

21) $\dfrac{21}{36} - \dfrac{11}{36} =$

22) $\dfrac{18}{27} - \dfrac{13}{27} =$

Add and Subtract Fractions with Like Denominators

✎ *Add fractions.*

1) $\dfrac{1}{2} + \dfrac{1}{2} =$

2) $\dfrac{1}{3} + \dfrac{2}{3} =$

3) $\dfrac{3}{6} + \dfrac{2}{6} =$

4) $\dfrac{5}{8} + \dfrac{2}{8} =$

5) $\dfrac{3}{9} + \dfrac{5}{9} =$

6) $\dfrac{4}{10} + \dfrac{1}{10} =$

7) $\dfrac{3}{7} + \dfrac{2}{7} =$

8) $\dfrac{3}{5} + \dfrac{2}{5} =$

9) $\dfrac{1}{12} + \dfrac{1}{12} =$

10) $\dfrac{16}{25} + \dfrac{5}{25} =$

✎ *Subtract fractions.*

11) $\dfrac{4}{5} - \dfrac{2}{5} =$

12) $\dfrac{5}{7} - \dfrac{3}{7} =$

13) $\dfrac{3}{4} - \dfrac{2}{4} =$

14) $\dfrac{8}{9} - \dfrac{3}{9} =$

15) $\dfrac{6}{14} - \dfrac{3}{14} =$

16) $\dfrac{4}{15} - \dfrac{1}{15} =$

17) $\dfrac{15}{16} - \dfrac{13}{16} =$

18) $\dfrac{25}{50} - \dfrac{20}{50} =$

19) $\dfrac{10}{21} - \dfrac{7}{21} =$

20) $\dfrac{12}{27} - \dfrac{8}{27} =$

Compare Sums and Differences of Fractions with Like Denominators

 *Evaluate and compare. Write < or > or =.*

1) $\frac{1}{2} + \frac{1}{2} \ \square \ \frac{1}{3}$

2) $\frac{1}{4} + \frac{2}{4} \ \square \ 1$

3) $\frac{1}{3} + \frac{1}{3} \ \square \ \frac{2}{3}$

4) $\frac{1}{4} + \frac{2}{4} \ \square \ \frac{1}{4}$

5) $\frac{3}{5} + \frac{2}{5} \ \square \ \frac{4}{5}$

6) $\frac{5}{7} - \frac{3}{7} \ \square \ \frac{6}{7}$

7) $\frac{9}{10} + \frac{7}{10} \ \square \ \frac{5}{10}$

8) $\frac{5}{9} - \frac{3}{9} \ \square \ \frac{7}{9}$

9) $\frac{10}{12} - \frac{5}{12} \ \square \ \frac{3}{12}$

10) $\frac{3}{8} + \frac{1}{8} \ \square \ \frac{1}{8}$

11) $\frac{10}{15} + \frac{4}{15} \ \square \ \frac{9}{15}$

12) $\frac{15}{18} - \frac{3}{18} \ \square \ \frac{17}{18}$

13) $\frac{17}{21} + \frac{4}{21} \ \square \ \frac{18}{21}$

14) $\frac{14}{16} - \frac{4}{16} \ \square \ \frac{12}{16}$

15) $\frac{27}{32} - \frac{11}{32} \ \square \ \frac{20}{32}$

16) $\frac{25}{30} + \frac{5}{30} \ \square \ \frac{15}{30}$

17) $\frac{25}{27} - \frac{3}{27} \ \square \ \frac{9}{27}$

18) $\frac{42}{45} - \frac{15}{45} \ \square \ \frac{30}{45}$

19) $\frac{32}{36} + \frac{15}{36} \ \square \ \frac{18}{36}$

20) $\frac{18}{42} + \frac{13}{42} \ \square \ \frac{30}{42}$

Add 3 or More Fractions with Like Denominators

✍ *Add fractions.*

1) $\dfrac{1}{3} + \dfrac{1}{3} + \dfrac{1}{3} =$

2) $\dfrac{2}{5} + \dfrac{1}{5} + \dfrac{1}{5} =$

3) $\dfrac{1}{6} + \dfrac{2}{6} + \dfrac{2}{6} =$

4) $\dfrac{4}{7} + \dfrac{2}{7} + \dfrac{1}{7} =$

5) $\dfrac{1}{5} + \dfrac{3}{5} + \dfrac{1}{5} =$

6) $\dfrac{3}{9} + \dfrac{3}{9} + \dfrac{1}{9} =$

7) $\dfrac{1}{4} + \dfrac{1}{4} + \dfrac{1}{4} =$

8) $\dfrac{7}{15} + \dfrac{3}{15} + \dfrac{4}{15} =$

9) $\dfrac{3}{12} + \dfrac{2}{12} + \dfrac{3}{12} =$

10) $\dfrac{4}{10} + \dfrac{2}{10} + \dfrac{1}{10} =$

11) $\dfrac{5}{18} + \dfrac{5}{18} + \dfrac{3}{18} =$

12) $\dfrac{5}{21} + \dfrac{11}{21} + \dfrac{3}{21} =$

13) $\dfrac{8}{20} + \dfrac{4}{20} + \dfrac{3}{20} =$

14) $\dfrac{2}{16} + \dfrac{5}{16} + \dfrac{8}{16} =$

15) $\dfrac{4}{25} + \dfrac{4}{25} + \dfrac{4}{25} =$

16) $\dfrac{12}{30} + \dfrac{7}{30} + \dfrac{5}{30} =$

17) $\dfrac{9}{27} + \dfrac{6}{27} + \dfrac{6}{27} =$

18) $\dfrac{3}{42} + \dfrac{5}{42} + \dfrac{6}{42} =$

19) $\dfrac{11}{32} + \dfrac{8}{32} + \dfrac{6}{32} =$

20) $\dfrac{9}{37} + \dfrac{11}{37} + \dfrac{10}{37} =$

21) $\dfrac{19}{45} + \dfrac{10}{45} + \dfrac{5}{45} =$

22) $\dfrac{22}{50} + \dfrac{12}{50} + \dfrac{11}{50} =$

Simplifying Fractions

✎ *Simplify each fraction to its lowest terms.*

1) $\frac{9}{18} =$

2) $\frac{8}{10} =$

3) $\frac{6}{8} =$

4) $\frac{5}{20} =$

5) $\frac{18}{24} =$

6) $\frac{6}{9} =$

7) $\frac{12}{15} =$

8) $\frac{4}{16} =$

9) $\frac{18}{36} =$

10) $\frac{6}{42} =$

11) $\frac{13}{39} =$

12) $\frac{21}{28} =$

13) $\frac{63}{77} =$

14) $\frac{36}{40} =$

15) $\frac{21}{63} =$

16) $\frac{30}{84} =$

17) $\frac{50}{125} =$

18) $\frac{72}{108} =$

19) $\frac{49}{112} =$

20) $\frac{240}{320} =$

21) $\frac{120}{150} =$

✎ *Solve each problem.*

22) Which of the following fractions equal to $\frac{4}{5}$? _____

   A. $\frac{64}{75}$ B. $\frac{92}{115}$ C. $\frac{60}{85}$ D. $\frac{160}{220}$

23) Which of the following fractions equal to $\frac{3}{7}$? _____

   A. $\frac{63}{147}$ B. $\frac{75}{182}$ C. $\frac{54}{140}$ D. $\frac{39}{98}$

24) Which of the following fractions equal to $\frac{2}{9}$? _____

   A. $\frac{84}{386}$ B. $\frac{52}{234}$ C. $\frac{96}{450}$ D. $\frac{112}{522}$

Add and Subtract Fractions with Unlike Denominators

✍ *Find the sum.*

1) $\dfrac{1}{3} + \dfrac{2}{3} =$

2) $\dfrac{1}{2} + \dfrac{1}{3} =$

3) $\dfrac{2}{5} + \dfrac{1}{2} =$

4) $\dfrac{3}{7} + \dfrac{2}{3} =$

5) $\dfrac{3}{4} + \dfrac{2}{5} =$

6) $\dfrac{3}{5} + \dfrac{1}{5} =$

7) $\dfrac{5}{9} + \dfrac{1}{2} =$

8) $\dfrac{3}{5} + \dfrac{3}{8} =$

9) $\dfrac{5}{9} + \dfrac{3}{7} =$

10) $\dfrac{5}{11} + \dfrac{1}{4} =$

11) $\dfrac{3}{7} + \dfrac{1}{6} =$

12) $\dfrac{3}{14} + \dfrac{3}{4} =$

✍ *Find the difference.*

13) $\dfrac{1}{2} - \dfrac{1}{3} =$

14) $\dfrac{4}{5} - \dfrac{2}{3} =$

15) $\dfrac{2}{3} - \dfrac{1}{6} =$

16) $\dfrac{3}{5} - \dfrac{1}{2} =$

17) $\dfrac{8}{9} - \dfrac{2}{5} =$

18) $\dfrac{4}{7} - \dfrac{1}{9} =$

19) $\dfrac{2}{5} - \dfrac{1}{4} =$

20) $\dfrac{5}{8} - \dfrac{2}{6} =$

21) $\dfrac{4}{15} - \dfrac{1}{10} =$

22) $\dfrac{7}{20} - \dfrac{1}{5} =$

23) $\dfrac{3}{18} - \dfrac{1}{12} =$

24) $\dfrac{9}{24} - \dfrac{3}{16} =$

25) $\dfrac{3}{7} - \dfrac{2}{5} =$

26) $\dfrac{5}{9} - \dfrac{1}{6} =$

27) $\dfrac{2}{5} - \dfrac{1}{10} =$

28) $\dfrac{5}{12} - \dfrac{2}{9} =$

29) $\dfrac{2}{13} - \dfrac{3}{7} =$

30) $\dfrac{4}{11} - \dfrac{5}{8} =$

Add Fractions with Denominators of 10 and 100

✎ *Add fractions.*

1) $\dfrac{5}{10} + \dfrac{20}{100} =$

2) $\dfrac{2}{10} + \dfrac{35}{100} =$

3) $\dfrac{25}{100} + \dfrac{6}{10} =$

4) $\dfrac{73}{100} + \dfrac{1}{10} =$

5) $\dfrac{68}{100} + \dfrac{2}{10} =$

6) $\dfrac{4}{10} + \dfrac{40}{100} =$

7) $\dfrac{80}{100} + \dfrac{1}{10} =$

8) $\dfrac{50}{100} + \dfrac{3}{10} =$

9) $\dfrac{59}{100} + \dfrac{3}{10} =$

10) $\dfrac{7}{10} + \dfrac{12}{100} =$

11) $\dfrac{9}{10} + \dfrac{10}{100} =$

12) $\dfrac{40}{100} + \dfrac{3}{10} =$

13) $\dfrac{36}{100} + \dfrac{4}{10} =$

14) $\dfrac{27}{100} + \dfrac{6}{10} =$

15) $\dfrac{55}{100} + \dfrac{3}{10} =$

16) $\dfrac{1}{10} + \dfrac{85}{100} =$

17) $\dfrac{17}{100} + \dfrac{6}{10} =$

18) $\dfrac{26}{100} + \dfrac{7}{10} =$

19) $\dfrac{45}{100} + \dfrac{4}{10} =$

20) $\dfrac{5}{10} + \dfrac{30}{100} =$

21) $\dfrac{56}{100} + \dfrac{2}{10} =$

22) $\dfrac{67}{100} + \dfrac{3}{10} =$

Add and Subtract Fractions with Denominators of 10, 100, and 1000

✍ *Evaluate fractions.*

1) $\dfrac{25}{100} - \dfrac{2}{10} =$

2) $\dfrac{45}{100} - \dfrac{3}{10} =$

3) $\dfrac{8}{10} - \dfrac{30}{100} =$

4) $\dfrac{6}{10} + \dfrac{27}{100} =$

5) $\dfrac{25}{100} + \dfrac{450}{1000} =$

6) $\dfrac{73}{100} - \dfrac{320}{1000} =$

7) $\dfrac{25}{100} + \dfrac{670}{1000} =$

8) $\dfrac{4}{10} + \dfrac{780}{1000} =$

9) $\dfrac{80}{100} - \dfrac{560}{1000} =$

10) $\dfrac{78}{100} - \dfrac{6}{10} =$

11) $\dfrac{820}{1000} + \dfrac{5}{10} =$

12) $\dfrac{67}{100} + \dfrac{240}{1000} =$

13) $\dfrac{7}{10} - \dfrac{12}{100} =$

14) $\dfrac{75}{100} - \dfrac{5}{10} =$

15) $\dfrac{70}{100} - \dfrac{3}{10} =$

16) $\dfrac{850}{1000} - \dfrac{5}{100} =$

17) $\dfrac{300}{1000} + \dfrac{12}{100} =$

18) $\dfrac{780}{1000} - \dfrac{6}{10} =$

19) $\dfrac{80}{100} - \dfrac{6}{10} =$

20) $\dfrac{50}{100} - \dfrac{210}{1000} =$

21) $\dfrac{350}{1000} - \dfrac{3}{10} =$

22) $\dfrac{85}{100} - \dfrac{450}{1000} =$

Answers of Worksheets – Chapter 14

Add Fractions with Like Denominators

1) 1

2) 1

3) $\dfrac{9}{8}$

4) $\dfrac{6}{4}$

5) $\dfrac{7}{10}$

6) $\dfrac{5}{7}$

7) $\dfrac{8}{5}$

8) $\dfrac{12}{14}$

9) $\dfrac{16}{18}$

10) $\dfrac{8}{12}$

11) $\dfrac{10}{13}$

12) $\dfrac{20}{25}$

13) 1

14) $\dfrac{9}{20}$

15) $\dfrac{12}{17}$

16) $\dfrac{33}{32}$

17) $\dfrac{22}{28}$

18) $\dfrac{12}{20}$

19) $\dfrac{35}{45}$

20) $\dfrac{26}{36}$

21) $\dfrac{31}{30}$

22) $\dfrac{33}{42}$

Subtract Fractions with Like Denominators

1) $\dfrac{2}{5}$

2) $\dfrac{1}{3}$

3) $\dfrac{3}{9}$

4) $\dfrac{2}{6}$

5) $\dfrac{1}{10}$

6) $\dfrac{2}{7}$

7) $\dfrac{2}{8}$

8) $\dfrac{2}{13}$

9) $\dfrac{3}{10}$

10) $\dfrac{1}{12}$

11) $\dfrac{6}{21}$

12) $\dfrac{6}{19}$

13) $\dfrac{3}{25}$

14) $\dfrac{1}{4}$

15) $\dfrac{13}{27}$

16) $\dfrac{12}{30}$

17) $\dfrac{5}{33}$

18) $\dfrac{10}{28}$

19) $\dfrac{20}{40}$

20) $\dfrac{2}{7}$

21) $\dfrac{10}{36}$

22) $\dfrac{5}{27}$

Add and Subtract Fractions with Like Denominators

1) 1

2) 1

3) $\dfrac{5}{6}$

4) $\dfrac{7}{8}$

5) $\dfrac{8}{9}$

6) $\dfrac{5}{10}$

7) $\dfrac{5}{7}$

8) 1

9) $\dfrac{2}{12}$

10) $\dfrac{21}{25}$

11) $\dfrac{2}{5}$

12) $\dfrac{2}{7}$

13) $\dfrac{1}{4}$

14) $\dfrac{5}{9}$

15) $\dfrac{3}{14}$

16) $\dfrac{3}{15}$

17) $\dfrac{2}{16}$

18) $\dfrac{5}{50}$

19) $\dfrac{3}{21}$

20) $\dfrac{4}{27}$

Compare Sums and Differences of Fractions with Like Denominators

1) $1 > \dfrac{1}{3}$

2) $\dfrac{3}{4} < 1$

3) $\dfrac{2}{3} = \dfrac{2}{3}$

4) $\dfrac{3}{4} > \dfrac{1}{4}$

5) $1 > \dfrac{4}{5}$

6) $\dfrac{2}{7} < \dfrac{6}{7}$

7) $\dfrac{16}{10} > \dfrac{5}{10}$

8) $\dfrac{2}{9} < \dfrac{7}{9}$

9) $\dfrac{5}{12} > \dfrac{3}{12}$

10) $\dfrac{4}{8} > \dfrac{1}{8}$

11) $\dfrac{14}{15} > \dfrac{9}{15}$

12) $\dfrac{12}{18} < \dfrac{17}{18}$

13) $1 > \dfrac{18}{21}$

14) $\dfrac{10}{16} < \dfrac{12}{16}$

15) $\dfrac{16}{32} < \dfrac{20}{32}$

16) $1 > \dfrac{15}{30}$

17) $\dfrac{22}{27} > \dfrac{9}{27}$

18) $\dfrac{27}{45} < \dfrac{30}{45}$

19) $\dfrac{47}{36} > \dfrac{18}{36}$

20) $\dfrac{31}{42} > \dfrac{30}{42}$

Add 3 or More Fractions with Like Denominators

1) 1

2) $\dfrac{4}{5}$

3) $\dfrac{5}{6}$

4) 1

5) 1

6) $\dfrac{7}{9}$

7) $\dfrac{3}{4}$

8) $\dfrac{14}{15}$

9) $\dfrac{8}{12}$

10) $\dfrac{7}{10}$

11) $\dfrac{13}{18}$

12) $\dfrac{19}{21}$

13) $\dfrac{15}{20}$

14) $\dfrac{15}{16}$

15) $\dfrac{12}{25}$

16) $\dfrac{24}{30}$

17) $\dfrac{21}{27}$

18) $\dfrac{14}{42}$

19) $\dfrac{25}{32}$

20) $\dfrac{30}{37}$

21) $\dfrac{34}{45}$

22) $\dfrac{45}{50}$

Simplifying Fractions

1) $\dfrac{1}{2}$

2) $\dfrac{4}{5}$

3) $\dfrac{3}{4}$

4) $\dfrac{1}{4}$

5) $\dfrac{3}{4}$

6) $\dfrac{2}{3}$

7) $\dfrac{4}{5}$

8) $\dfrac{1}{4}$

9) $\dfrac{1}{2}$

10) $\dfrac{1}{7}$

11) $\dfrac{1}{3}$

12) $\dfrac{3}{4}$

13) $\dfrac{9}{11}$

14) $\dfrac{9}{10}$

15) $\dfrac{1}{3}$

16) $\dfrac{5}{14}$

17) $\dfrac{2}{5}$

18) $\dfrac{2}{3}$

19) $\dfrac{7}{16}$

20) $\dfrac{3}{4}$

21) $\dfrac{4}{5}$

22) B

23) A

24) B

Add and Subtract fractions with unlike denominators

1) $\dfrac{3}{3} = 1$

2) $\dfrac{5}{6}$

3) $\dfrac{9}{10}$

4) $\dfrac{23}{21}$

5) $\dfrac{23}{20}$

6) $\dfrac{4}{5}$

7) $\dfrac{19}{18}$

8) $\dfrac{39}{40}$

9) $\dfrac{62}{63}$

10) $\dfrac{31}{44}$

11) $\dfrac{25}{42}$

12) $\dfrac{27}{28}$

13) $\dfrac{1}{6}$

14) $\dfrac{2}{15}$

15) $\dfrac{1}{2}$

16) $\dfrac{1}{10}$

17) $\dfrac{22}{45}$

18) $\dfrac{29}{63}$

19) $\dfrac{3}{20}$

20) $\dfrac{7}{24}$

21) $\dfrac{1}{6}$

22) $\dfrac{3}{20}$

23) $\dfrac{1}{12}$

24) $\dfrac{3}{16}$

25) $\frac{1}{35}$

26) $\frac{7}{18}$

27) $\frac{3}{10}$

28) $\frac{7}{36}$

29) $-\frac{25}{91}$

30) $-\frac{15}{88}$

Add fractions with denominators of 10 and 100

1) $\frac{7}{10}$

2) $\frac{11}{20}$

3) $\frac{17}{20}$

4) $\frac{83}{100}$

5) $\frac{22}{25}$

6) $\frac{4}{5}$

7) $\frac{9}{10}$

8) $\frac{4}{5}$

9) $\frac{89}{100}$

10) $\frac{41}{50}$

11) 1

12) $\frac{7}{10}$

13) $\frac{19}{25}$

14) $\frac{87}{100}$

15) $\frac{17}{20}$

16) $\frac{19}{20}$

17) $\frac{77}{100}$

18) $\frac{24}{25}$

19) $\frac{17}{20}$

20) $\frac{4}{5}$

21) $\frac{19}{25}$

22) $\frac{97}{100}$

Add and subtract fractions with denominators of 10, 100, and 1000

1) $\frac{1}{20}$

2) $\frac{3}{20}$

3) $\frac{50}{100}$

4) $\frac{87}{100}$

5) $\frac{7}{10}$

6) $\frac{41}{100}$

7) $\frac{23}{25}$

8) $\frac{59}{50}$

9) $\frac{6}{25}$

10) $\frac{9}{50}$

11) $\frac{33}{25}$

12) $\frac{91}{100}$

13) $\frac{29}{50}$

14) $\frac{1}{4}$

15) $\frac{2}{5}$

16) $\frac{4}{5}$

17) $\frac{21}{50}$

18) $\frac{9}{50}$

19) $\frac{1}{5}$

20) $\frac{29}{100}$

21) $\frac{1}{20}$

22) $\frac{2}{5}$

Chapter 15:
Mixed Numbers

Topics that you'll practice in this chapter:

- ✓ Fractions to Mixed Numbers
- ✓ Mixed Numbers to Fractions
- ✓ Add and Subtract Mixed Numbers

Fractions to Mixed Numbers

✎ *Convert fractions to mixed numbers.*

1) $\dfrac{4}{3} =$

2) $\dfrac{3}{2} =$

3) $\dfrac{5}{3} =$

4) $\dfrac{7}{2} =$

5) $\dfrac{8}{5} =$

6) $\dfrac{7}{3} =$

7) $\dfrac{9}{4} =$

8) $\dfrac{12}{5} =$

9) $\dfrac{13}{9} =$

10) $\dfrac{18}{7} =$

11) $\dfrac{15}{7} =$

12) $\dfrac{19}{6} =$

13) $\dfrac{13}{5} =$

14) $\dfrac{37}{5} =$

15) $\dfrac{21}{6} =$

16) $\dfrac{41}{10} =$

17) $\dfrac{11}{2} =$

18) $\dfrac{56}{10} =$

19) $\dfrac{20}{12} =$

20) $\dfrac{9}{5} =$

21) $\dfrac{19}{5} =$

22) $\dfrac{27}{10} =$

23) $\dfrac{10}{6} =$

24) $\dfrac{17}{8} =$

25) $\dfrac{7}{2} =$

26) $\dfrac{39}{4} =$

27) $\dfrac{72}{10} =$

28) $\dfrac{13}{3} =$

29) $\dfrac{45}{8} =$

30) $\dfrac{27}{5} =$

Mixed Numbers to Fractions

✎ *Convert to fraction.*

1) $2\frac{1}{2} =$

2) $1\frac{2}{3} =$

3) $1\frac{1}{3} =$

4) $2\frac{1}{4} =$

5) $3\frac{2}{5} =$

6) $4\frac{1}{4} =$

7) $5\frac{2}{3} =$

8) $1\frac{2}{7} =$

9) $3\frac{2}{9} =$

10) $1\frac{2}{6} =$

11) $2\frac{2}{3} =$

12) $5\frac{1}{3} =$

13) $6\frac{4}{5} =$

14) $2\frac{3}{4} =$

15) $2\frac{5}{7} =$

16) $3\frac{5}{9} =$

17) $2\frac{9}{10} =$

18) $7\frac{5}{6} =$

19) $6\frac{11}{12} =$

20) $8\frac{9}{20} =$

21) $8\frac{2}{5} =$

22) $5\frac{4}{5} =$

23) $9\frac{1}{6} =$

24) $3\frac{3}{4} =$

25) $5\frac{2}{8} =$

26) $10\frac{2}{3} =$

27) $12\frac{3}{4} =$

28) $14\frac{6}{7} =$

29) $3\frac{7}{11} =$

30) $6\frac{5}{11} =$

31) $7\frac{6}{15} =$

32) $9\frac{11}{21} =$

33) $5\frac{15}{27} =$

Add and Subtract Mixed Numbers

✎ *Find the sum.*

1) $2\frac{1}{2} + 1\frac{1}{3} =$

2) $6\frac{1}{2} + 3\frac{1}{2} =$

3) $2\frac{3}{8} + 3\frac{1}{8} =$

4) $4\frac{1}{2} + 1\frac{1}{4} =$

5) $1\frac{3}{7} + 1\frac{5}{14} =$

6) $6\frac{5}{12} + 3\frac{3}{4} =$

7) $5\frac{1}{2} + 8\frac{3}{4} =$

8) $3\frac{7}{8} + 3\frac{1}{3} =$

9) $3\frac{3}{9} + 7\frac{6}{11} =$

10) $7\frac{5}{12} + 4\frac{3}{10} =$

✎ *Find the difference.*

11) $3\frac{1}{3} - 1\frac{1}{3} =$

12) $4\frac{1}{2} - 3\frac{1}{2} =$

13) $5\frac{1}{2} - 2\frac{1}{4} =$

14) $6\frac{1}{6} - 5\frac{1}{3} =$

15) $8\frac{1}{2} - 1\frac{1}{10} =$

16) $9\frac{1}{2} - 2\frac{1}{4} =$

17) $9\frac{1}{5} - 5\frac{1}{6} =$

18) $14\frac{3}{10} - 13\frac{1}{3} =$

19) $19\frac{2}{3} - 11\frac{5}{8} =$

20) $20\frac{3}{4} - 14\frac{2}{3} =$

21) $2\frac{1}{2} - 1\frac{1}{5} =$

22) $3\frac{1}{6} - 1\frac{1}{10} =$

23) $16\frac{2}{7} - 11\frac{2}{3} =$

24) $15\frac{1}{7} - 10\frac{1}{8} =$

25) $12\frac{3}{4} - 7\frac{1}{3} =$

26) $15\frac{2}{5} - 5\frac{2}{3} =$

Multiplying and Dividing Mixed Numbers

✎ *Find the product.*

1) $4\frac{1}{3} \times 2\frac{1}{5} =$

2) $3\frac{1}{2} \times 3\frac{1}{4} =$

3) $5\frac{2}{5} \times 2\frac{1}{3} =$

4) $2\frac{1}{2} \times 1\frac{2}{9} =$

5) $3\frac{4}{7} \times 2\frac{3}{5} =$

6) $7\frac{2}{3} \times 2\frac{2}{3} =$

7) $9\frac{8}{9} \times 8\frac{3}{4} =$

8) $2\frac{4}{7} \times 5\frac{2}{9} =$

9) $5\frac{2}{5} \times 2\frac{3}{5} =$

10) $3\frac{5}{7} \times 3\frac{5}{6} =$

✎ *Find the quotient.*

11) $1\frac{2}{3} \div 3\frac{1}{3} =$

12) $2\frac{1}{4} \div 1\frac{1}{2} =$

13) $10\frac{1}{2} \div 1\frac{2}{3} =$

14) $3\frac{1}{6} \div 4\frac{2}{3} =$

15) $4\frac{1}{8} \div 2\frac{1}{2} =$

16) $2\frac{1}{10} \div 2\frac{3}{5} =$

17) $1\frac{4}{11} \div 1\frac{1}{4} =$

18) $9\frac{1}{2} \div 9\frac{2}{3} =$

19) $8\frac{3}{4} \div 2\frac{2}{5} =$

20) $12\frac{1}{2} \div 9\frac{1}{3} =$

21) $2\frac{1}{8} \div 1\frac{1}{2} =$

22) $1\frac{1}{10} \div 1\frac{3}{5} =$

23) $5\frac{2}{5} \div 1\frac{3}{4} =$

24) $5\frac{1}{2} \div 2\frac{2}{3} =$

25) $3\frac{3}{4} \div 1\frac{1}{5} =$

26) $3\frac{1}{2} \div 1\frac{1}{3} =$

Answers of Worksheets – Chapter 15

Fractions to Mixed Numbers

1) $1\frac{1}{3}$

2) $1\frac{1}{2}$

3) $1\frac{2}{3}$

4) $3\frac{1}{2}$

5) $1\frac{3}{5}$

6) $2\frac{1}{3}$

7) $2\frac{1}{4}$

8) $2\frac{2}{5}$

9) $1\frac{4}{9}$

10) $2\frac{4}{7}$

11) $2\frac{1}{7}$

12) $3\frac{1}{6}$

13) $2\frac{3}{5}$

14) $7\frac{2}{5}$

15) $3\frac{1}{2}$

16) $4\frac{1}{10}$

17) $5\frac{1}{2}$

18) $5\frac{3}{5}$

19) $1\frac{2}{3}$

20) $1\frac{4}{5}$

21) $3\frac{4}{5}$

22) $2\frac{7}{10}$

23) $1\frac{2}{3}$

24) $2\frac{1}{8}$

25) $3\frac{1}{2}$

26) $9\frac{3}{4}$

27) $7\frac{1}{5}$

28) $4\frac{1}{3}$

29) $5\frac{5}{8}$

30) $5\frac{2}{5}$

Mixed Numbers to Fractions

1) $\frac{5}{2}$

2) $\frac{5}{3}$

3) $\frac{4}{3}$

4) $\frac{9}{4}$

5) $\frac{17}{5}$

6) $\frac{17}{4}$

7) $\frac{17}{3}$

8) $\frac{9}{7}$

9) $\frac{29}{9}$

10) $\frac{4}{3}$

11) $\frac{8}{3}$

12) $\frac{16}{3}$

13) $\frac{34}{5}$

14) $\frac{11}{4}$

15) $\frac{19}{7}$

16) $\frac{32}{9}$

17) $\frac{29}{10}$

18) $\frac{47}{6}$

19) $\frac{83}{12}$

20) $\frac{169}{20}$

21) $\frac{42}{5}$

22) $\frac{29}{5}$

23) $\frac{55}{6}$

24) $\frac{21}{4}$

25) $\frac{15}{4}$ 28) $\frac{104}{7}$ 31) $\frac{37}{5}$

26) $\frac{32}{3}$ 29) $\frac{40}{11}$ 32) $\frac{200}{21}$

27) $\frac{51}{4}$ 30) $\frac{71}{11}$ 33) $\frac{50}{9}$

Add and Subtract Mixed Numbers with Like Denominators

1) $3\frac{5}{6}$ 10) $11\frac{43}{60}$ 19) $8\frac{1}{24}$

2) 10 11) 2 20) $6\frac{1}{12}$

3) $5\frac{1}{2}$ 12) 1 21) $\frac{13}{10}$

4) $5\frac{3}{4}$ 13) $3\frac{1}{4}$ 22) $2\frac{1}{15}$

5) $2\frac{11}{14}$ 14) $\frac{5}{6}$ 23) $4\frac{13}{21}$

6) $10\frac{1}{6}$ 15) $7\frac{2}{5}$ 24) $5\frac{1}{56}$

7) $14\frac{1}{4}$ 16) $7\frac{1}{4}$ 25) $5\frac{5}{12}$

8) $7\frac{5}{24}$ 17) $4\frac{1}{30}$ 26) $9\frac{11}{15}$

9) $10\frac{29}{33}$ 18) $\frac{29}{30}$

Adding and Subtracting Mixed Numbers

1) $3\frac{5}{6}$ 10) $11\frac{43}{60}$ 19) $8\frac{1}{24}$

2) 10 11) 2 20) $6\frac{1}{12}$

3) $5\frac{1}{2}$ 12) 1 21) $\frac{13}{10}$

4) $5\frac{3}{4}$ 13) $3\frac{1}{4}$ 22) $2\frac{1}{15}$

5) $2\frac{11}{14}$ 14) $\frac{5}{6}$ 23) $4\frac{13}{21}$

6) $10\frac{1}{6}$ 15) $7\frac{2}{5}$ 24) $5\frac{1}{56}$

7) $14\frac{1}{4}$ 16) $7\frac{1}{4}$ 25) $5\frac{5}{12}$

8) $7\frac{5}{24}$ 17) $4\frac{1}{30}$ 26) $9\frac{11}{15}$

9) $10\frac{29}{33}$ 18) $\frac{29}{30}$

Chapter 16: Decimal

Topics that you'll practice in this chapter:

- ✓ Decimal Place Value
- ✓ Ordering and Comparing Decimals
- ✓ Decimal Addition
- ✓ Decimal Subtraction

Decimal Place Value

✍ *Identify the place value of the underlined digits.*

1) 1,12<u>2</u>.25

2) 2,321.3<u>2</u>

3) 4,258.91

4) 6,3<u>7</u>2.67

5) 7,131.<u>9</u>8

6) <u>5</u>,442.73

7) 1,841.8<u>9</u>

8) 5,995.<u>7</u>6

9) 8,<u>9</u>82.55

10) 1,24<u>9</u>.21

11) 4,31<u>6</u>.50

12) 9,1<u>9</u>1.99

13) <u>9</u>,112.51

14) 8,435.2<u>7</u>

15) 1,6<u>6</u>2.24

16) 1,14<u>8</u>.44

17) 9,989.<u>6</u>9

18) 3,<u>1</u>55.91

✍ *What is the value of the selected digits?*

19) 3,122.3<u>1</u>

20) 1,3<u>1</u>8.66

21) 6,352.<u>2</u>5

22) 3,<u>7</u>39.16

23) 4,9<u>3</u>6.78

24) 7,62<u>5</u>.86

25) 9,313.4<u>5</u>

26) <u>2</u>,168.82

27) 8,<u>4</u>51.76

28) 2,153.<u>2</u>3

Ordering and Comparing Decimals

✎ *Write the correct comparison symbol (>, < or =).*

1) 0.50 ☐ 0.050

2) 0.025 ☐ 0.25

3) 2.060 ☐ 2.07

4) 1.75 ☐ 1.07

5) 4.04 ☐ 0.440

6) 3.05 ☐ 3.5

7) 5.05 ☐ 5.050

8) 1.02 ☐ 1.1

9) 2.45 ☐ 2.125

10) 0.932 ☐ 0.0932

11) 3.15 ☐ 3.150

12) 0.718 ☐ 0.89

13) 7.060 ☐ 7.60

14) 3.59 ☐ 3.129

15) 4.33 ☐ 4.319

16) 2.25 ☐ 2.250

17) 1.95 ☐ 1.095

18) 8.051 ☐ 8.50

✎ *Order each set of integers from least to greatest.*

19) 0.4, 0.54, 0.23, 0.87, 0.36   ___, ___, ___, ___, ___, ___

20) 1.2, 2.4, 1.97, 3.65, 1.80   ___, ___, ___, ___, ___, ___

21) 2.3, 1.2, 1.9, 0.67, 0.34   ___, ___, ___, ___, ___, ___

22) 1.7, 1.2, 3.2, 4.2, 1.34, 3.55   ___, ___, ___, ___, ___, ___

Adding and Subtracting Decimals

✎ **Add and subtract decimals.**

1)
$$\begin{array}{r} 31.13 \\ -\ 11.45 \\ \hline \end{array}$$

4)
$$\begin{array}{r} 56.67 \\ -\ 44.39 \\ \hline \end{array}$$

7)
$$\begin{array}{r} 66.24 \\ -\ 23.11 \\ \hline \end{array}$$

2)
$$\begin{array}{r} 35.25 \\ +\ 24.47 \\ \hline \end{array}$$

5)
$$\begin{array}{r} 71.47 \\ +\ 16.25 \\ \hline \end{array}$$

8)
$$\begin{array}{r} 39.75 \\ +\ 12.85 \\ \hline \end{array}$$

3)
$$\begin{array}{r} 73.50 \\ +\ 22.78 \\ \hline \end{array}$$

6)
$$\begin{array}{r} 68.99 \\ -\ 53.61 \\ \hline \end{array}$$

9)
$$\begin{array}{r} 229.25 \\ -\ 84.67 \\ \hline \end{array}$$

✎ **Find the missing number.**

10) ___ + 2.5 = 3.9

11) 1.7 + ___ = 4.98

12) 5.25 + ___ = 7

13) 6.55 − ___ = 2.45

14) ___ − 3.98 = 5.32

15) ___ − 11.67 = 14.48

16) 12.35 + ___ = 14.78

17) ___ − 23.89 = 13.90

18) ___ + 17.28 = 19.56

19) 77.90 + ___ = 102.60

Multiplying and Dividing Decimals

✍ *Find the product.*

1) $0.5 \times 0.4 =$

2) $2.5 \times 0.2 =$

3) $1.25 \times 0.5 =$

4) $0.75 \times 0.2 =$

5) $1.92 \times 0.8 =$

6) $0.55 \times 0.4 =$

7) $3.24 \times 1.2 =$

8) $12.5 \times 4.2 =$

9) $22.6 \times 8.2 =$

10) $17.2 \times 4.5 =$

11) $25.1 \times 12.5 =$

12) $33.2 \times 2.2 =$

✍ *Find the quotient.*

13) $1.67 \div 100 =$

14) $52.2 \div 1,000 =$

15) $4.2 \div 2 =$

16) $8.6 \div 0.5 =$

17) $12.6 \div 0.2 =$

18) $16.5 \div 5 =$

19) $13.25 \div 100 =$

20) $25.6 \div 0.4 =$

21) $28.24 \div 0.1 =$

22) $34.16 \div 0.25 =$

23) $44.28 \div 0.5 =$

24) $38.78 \div 0.02 =$

Answers of Worksheets – Chapter 16

Decimal Place Value

1) one
2) hundredths
3) hundredths
4) tenths
5) tenths
6) thousands
7) hundredths
8) tenths
9) hundredths
10) ones
11) one
12) tenths
13) thousands
14) hundredths
15) one
16) tenths
17) hundredths
18) 0.01
19) 10
20) 0.2
21) 700
22) 30
23) 5
24) 0.05
25) 2,000
26) 400
27) 0.2

Order and Comparing Decimals

1) $>$
2) $<$
3) $<$
4) $>$
5) $>$
6) $<$
7) $=$
8) $<$
9) $>$
10) $>$
11) $=$
12) $<$
13) $<$
14) $>$
15) $>$
16) $=$
17) $>$
18) $<$
19) 0.23, 0.36, 0.4, 0.54, 0.87
20) 1.2, 1.80, 1.97, 2.4, 3.65
21) 0.34, 0.67, 1.2, 1.9, 2.3
22) 1.2, 1.34, 1.7, 3.2, 3.55, 4.2

Adding and Subtracting Decimals

1) 19.68
2) 59.72
3) 96.28
4) 12.28
5) 87.72
6) 15.38
7) 43.13
8) 52.60
9) 144.58
10) 1.4
11) 3.28
12) 1.75
13) 4.1
14) 9.3
15) 26.15
16) 2.43
17) 37.79
18) 2.28
19) 24.7

Multiplying and Dividing Decimals

1) 0.2
2) 0.5
3) 0.625
4) 0.15
5) 1.536
6) 0.22
7) 3.888
8) 52.5
9) 185.32
10) 77.4
11) 313.75
12) 73.04

13) 0.0167

14) 0.0522

15) 2.1

16) 4.3

17) 63

18) 3.3

19) 0.1325

20) 64

21) 282.4

22) 136.64

23) 88.56

1,939

SSAT Lower Level Math Practice Tests

The SSAT, or Secondary School Admissions Test, is a standardized test to help determine admission to private elementary, middle and high schools.

There are currently three Levels of the SSAT:

- ✓ Lower Level (for students in 3rd and 4th grade)
- ✓ Middle Level (for students in 5th-7th grade)
- ✓ Upper Level (for students in 8th-11th grade)

There are four sections on the SSAT Lower Level Test:

- ✓ Quantitative section: 30 questions, 30 minutes.
- ✓ Verbal section: 30 questions, 20 minutes.
- ✓ Reading section: 7 short passages, 28 questions, 30 minutes.
- ✓ Writing sample: 15 minutes to write a short passage

In this book, we have reviewed mathematics topics being tested on the quantitative (math) section of the SSAT Middle Level. In this section, there are two complete SSAT Lower Level Quantitative Tests. Let your student take these tests to see what score they will be able to receive on a real SSAT Lower Level test.

Good luck!

Time to Test

Time to refine your skill with a practice examination

Take two practice SSAT Lower Level Mathematics Tests to simulate the test day experience. After you've finished, score your test using the answer key.

Before You Start

- You'll need a pencil and a timer to take the test.

- After you've finished the test, review the answer key to see where you went wrong.

- Use the answer sheet provided to record your answers. (You can cut it out or photocopy it)

- You will receive 1 point for every correct answer. You won't receive any point for wrong or skipped answers.

Calculators are NOT permitted for the SSAT Lower Level Test

Good Luck!

SSAT Lower Level Mathematics Practice Tests Answer Sheet

SSAT Lower Level Practice Test 1

1	Ⓐ Ⓑ Ⓒ Ⓓ Ⓔ	11	Ⓐ Ⓑ Ⓒ Ⓓ Ⓔ	21	Ⓐ Ⓑ Ⓒ Ⓓ Ⓔ
2	Ⓐ Ⓑ Ⓒ Ⓓ Ⓔ	12	Ⓐ Ⓑ Ⓒ Ⓓ Ⓔ	22	Ⓐ Ⓑ Ⓒ Ⓓ Ⓔ
3	Ⓐ Ⓑ Ⓒ Ⓓ Ⓔ	13	Ⓐ Ⓑ Ⓒ Ⓓ Ⓔ	23	Ⓐ Ⓑ Ⓒ Ⓓ Ⓔ
4	Ⓐ Ⓑ Ⓒ Ⓓ Ⓔ	14	Ⓐ Ⓑ Ⓒ Ⓓ Ⓔ	24	Ⓐ Ⓑ Ⓒ Ⓓ Ⓔ
5	Ⓐ Ⓑ Ⓒ Ⓓ Ⓔ	15	Ⓐ Ⓑ Ⓒ Ⓓ Ⓔ	25	Ⓐ Ⓑ Ⓒ Ⓓ Ⓔ
6	Ⓐ Ⓑ Ⓒ Ⓓ Ⓔ	16	Ⓐ Ⓑ Ⓒ Ⓓ Ⓔ	26	Ⓐ Ⓑ Ⓒ Ⓓ Ⓔ
7	Ⓐ Ⓑ Ⓒ Ⓓ Ⓔ	17	Ⓐ Ⓑ Ⓒ Ⓓ Ⓔ	27	Ⓐ Ⓑ Ⓒ Ⓓ Ⓔ
8	Ⓐ Ⓑ Ⓒ Ⓓ Ⓔ	18	Ⓐ Ⓑ Ⓒ Ⓓ Ⓔ	28	Ⓐ Ⓑ Ⓒ Ⓓ Ⓔ
9	Ⓐ Ⓑ Ⓒ Ⓓ Ⓔ	19	Ⓐ Ⓑ Ⓒ Ⓓ Ⓔ	29	Ⓐ Ⓑ Ⓒ Ⓓ Ⓔ
10	Ⓐ Ⓑ Ⓒ Ⓓ Ⓔ	20	Ⓐ Ⓑ Ⓒ Ⓓ Ⓔ	30	Ⓐ Ⓑ Ⓒ Ⓓ Ⓔ

SSAT Lower Level Practice Test 2

1	Ⓐ Ⓑ Ⓒ Ⓓ Ⓔ	11	Ⓐ Ⓑ Ⓒ Ⓓ Ⓔ	21	Ⓐ Ⓑ Ⓒ Ⓓ Ⓔ
2	Ⓐ Ⓑ Ⓒ Ⓓ Ⓔ	12	Ⓐ Ⓑ Ⓒ Ⓓ Ⓔ	22	Ⓐ Ⓑ Ⓒ Ⓓ Ⓔ
3	Ⓐ Ⓑ Ⓒ Ⓓ Ⓔ	13	Ⓐ Ⓑ Ⓒ Ⓓ Ⓔ	23	Ⓐ Ⓑ Ⓒ Ⓓ Ⓔ
4	Ⓐ Ⓑ Ⓒ Ⓓ Ⓔ	14	Ⓐ Ⓑ Ⓒ Ⓓ Ⓔ	24	Ⓐ Ⓑ Ⓒ Ⓓ Ⓔ
5	Ⓐ Ⓑ Ⓒ Ⓓ Ⓔ	15	Ⓐ Ⓑ Ⓒ Ⓓ Ⓔ	25	Ⓐ Ⓑ Ⓒ Ⓓ Ⓔ
6	Ⓐ Ⓑ Ⓒ Ⓓ Ⓔ	16	Ⓐ Ⓑ Ⓒ Ⓓ Ⓔ	26	Ⓐ Ⓑ Ⓒ Ⓓ Ⓔ
7	Ⓐ Ⓑ Ⓒ Ⓓ Ⓔ	17	Ⓐ Ⓑ Ⓒ Ⓓ Ⓔ	27	Ⓐ Ⓑ Ⓒ Ⓓ Ⓔ
8	Ⓐ Ⓑ Ⓒ Ⓓ Ⓔ	18	Ⓐ Ⓑ Ⓒ Ⓓ Ⓔ	28	Ⓐ Ⓑ Ⓒ Ⓓ Ⓔ
9	Ⓐ Ⓑ Ⓒ Ⓓ Ⓔ	19	Ⓐ Ⓑ Ⓒ Ⓓ Ⓔ	29	Ⓐ Ⓑ Ⓒ Ⓓ Ⓔ
10	Ⓐ Ⓑ Ⓒ Ⓓ Ⓔ	20	Ⓐ Ⓑ Ⓒ Ⓓ Ⓔ	30	Ⓐ Ⓑ Ⓒ Ⓓ Ⓔ

SSAT Lower Level

Quantitative Practice Test 1

30 questions

Total time for this test: 30 Minutes

You may NOT use a calculator for this test.

1) In the following figure, the shaded squares are what fractional part of the whole set of squares?

   A. $\frac{1}{2}$

   B. $\frac{5}{8}$

   C. $\frac{2}{3}$

   D. $\frac{3}{5}$

   E. $\frac{6}{11}$

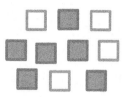

2) Which of the following is greater than $\frac{12}{8}$?

   A. $\frac{1}{2}$

   B. $\frac{5}{2}$

   C. $\frac{3}{4}$

   D. 1

   E. 1.4

3) If $\frac{1}{3}$ of a number is greater than 8, the number must be .....

   A. Less than 4

   B. Equal to 16

   C. Equal to 24

   D. Greater than 24

   E. Equal to 32

4) If $4 \times (M + N) = 20$ and M is greater than 0, then N could Not be .....
   A. 1
   B. 2
   C. 3
   D. 4
   E. 5

5) Which of the following is closest to 5.03?
   A. 6
   B. 5.5
   C. 5
   D. 5.4
   E. 6.5

6) At a Zoo, the ratio of lions to tigers is 10 to 6. Which of the following could NOT be the total number of lions and tigers in the zoo?
   A. 64
   B. 80
   C. 98
   D. 104
   E. 160

7) In the multiplication bellow, A represents which digit?
$$14 \times 3A2 = 4,788$$
   A. 2
   B. 3
   C. 4
   D. 6
   E. 8

8) If N is an even number, which of the following is always an odd number?

   A. $\frac{N}{2}$

   B. $N + 4$

   C. $2N$

   D. $(2 \times N) + 2$

   E. $N + 1$

9) $8.9 - 4.08$ is closest to which of the following.

   A. 4.1

   B. 4.8

   C. 6

   D. 8

   E. 13

$$x = 2,456 \qquad y = 259$$

10) Numbers x and y are shown above. How many times larger is the value of digit 5 in the number x, than the value of digit 5 in the number y?

   A. 1

   B. 10

   C. 100

   D. 1,000

   E. 10,000

11) If 5 added to a number, the sum is 20. If the same number added to 25, the answer is

   A. 30

   B. 35

   C. 40

   D. 45

   E. 50

12) $\dfrac{2+5+6\times1+1}{3+5} = ?$

   A. $\dfrac{15}{8}$

   B. $\dfrac{4}{8}$

   C. $\dfrac{7}{4}$

   D. $\dfrac{6}{8}$

   E. $\dfrac{10}{8}$

13) What is the Area of the square shown in the following square?

   A. 2

   B. 4

   C. 6

   D. 8

   E. 10

14) If 20 can be divided by both 4 and x without leaving a remainder, then 20 can also be divided by which of the following?

   A. $x + 4$

   B. $2x - 4$

   C. $x - 2$

   D. $x \times 4$

   E. $x + 1$

15) Use the equations below to answer the question:

$$x - 12 = 18$$
$$16 + y = 21$$

   What is the value of $x + y$?

   A. 9

   B. 10

   C. 11

   D. 12

   E. 14

16) Which of the following expressions has the same value as $\frac{5}{4} \times \frac{6}{2}$?

    A. $\frac{6 \times 3}{4}$

    B. $\frac{6 \times 2}{4}$

    C. $\frac{5 \times 6}{4}$

    D. $\frac{5 \times 3}{4}$

    E. $\frac{8 \times 3}{4}$

17) When 5 is added to three times number N, the result is 41. Then N is ….

    A. 11

    B. 12

    C. 14

    D. 16

    E. 18

18) At noon, the temperature was 15 degrees. By midnight, it had dropped another 20 degrees. What was the temperature at midnight?

    A. 10 degrees above zero

    B. 10 degrees below zero

    C. 5 degrees above zero

    D. 5 degrees below zero

    E. 15 degrees below zero

19) If a triangle has a base of 5 cm and a height of 8 cm, what is the area of the triangle?

    A. $15cm^2$

    B. $20cm^2$

    C. $40cm^2$

    D. $45cm^2$

    E. $50cm^2$

20) Which formula would you use to find the area of a square?
   A. $length \times width \times height$
   B. $\frac{1}{2}base \times height$
   C. $length \times width$
   D. $side \times side$
   E. $\frac{1}{2}(length \times width \times heigt)$

21) What is the next number in this sequence?   2, 5, 9, 14, 20, …
   A. 27
   B. 26
   C. 25
   D. 21
   E. 20

22) What is the average of the following numbers?   6, 10, 12, 23, 45
   A. 19
   B. 19.2
   C. 19.5
   D. 20
   E. 25

23) If there are 8 red balls and 12 blue balls in a basket, what is the probability that John will pick out a red ball from the basket?
   A. $\frac{18}{10}$
   B. $\frac{2}{5}$
   C. $\frac{2}{10}$
   D. $\frac{3}{5}$
   E. $\frac{20}{10}$

24) How many lines of symmetry does an equilateral triangle have?

    A. 5

    B. 4

    C. 3

    D. 2

    E. 1

25) What is %10 of 200?

    A. 10

    B. 20

    C. 30

    D. 40

    E. 50

26) Which of the following statement is False?

    A. $2 \times 2 = 4$

    B. $(4 + 1) \times 5 = 25$

    C. $6 \div (3 - 1) = 1$

    D. $6 \times (4 - 2) = 12$

    E. $(10 + 23) \times 10 = 330$

27) If all the sides in the following figure are of equal length and length of one side is 4, what is the perimeter of the figure?

    A. 15

    B. 18

    C. 20

    D. 24

    E. 28

28) $\frac{4}{5} - \frac{3}{5} = ?$

    A. 0.3

    B. 0.35

    C. 0.2

    D. 0.25

    E. 0.1

29) If $N = 2$ and $\frac{64}{N} + 4 = \square$, then $\square = \ldots$
   A. 30
   B. 32
   C. 34
   D. 36
   E. 38

30) Four people can paint 4 houses in 10 days. How many people are needed to paint 8 houses in 5 days?
   A. 6
   B. 8
   C. 12
   D. 16
   E. 20

IF YOU FINISH BEFORE TIME IS CALLED, YOU MAY CHECK YOUR WORK ON THIS SECTION ONLY. DO NOT TURN TO OTHER SECTION IN THE TEST. STOP

SSAT Lower Level

Quantitative Practice Test 2

30 questions

Total time for this test: 30 Minutes

You may NOT use a calculator for this test.

1) $\frac{8}{2} - \frac{3}{2} = ?$

   A. 1
   B. 1.5
   C. 2
   D. 2.5
   E. 3

2) If $48 = 3 \times N + 12$, then $N = \ldots$
   A. 8
   B. 12
   C. 14
   D. 15
   E. 20

3) The area of each square in the following shape is $8cm^2$. What is the area of shaded squares?
   A) $40cm^2$
   B) $42cm^2$
   C) $44cm^2$
   D) $45cm^2$
   E) $46cm^2$

4) What is the value of x in the following math equation?
   $$\frac{x}{15} + 9 = 11$$

   A) 15
   B) 20
   C) 25
   D) 35
   E) 30

5) When 3 is added to four times a number N, the result is 23. Which of the following equations represents this statement?
   A. $4 + 3N = 23$
   B. $23N + 4 = 3$
   C. $4N + 3 = 23$
   D. $4N + 23 = 3$
   E. $3N + 23 = 4$

6) When 78 is divided by 5, the remainder is the same as when 45 is divided by
   A. 2
   B. 4
   C. 5
   D. 7
   E. 9

7) John has 2,400 cards and Max has 606 cards. How many more cards does John have than Max?
   A. 1,794
   B. 1,798
   C. 1,812
   D. 1,828
   E. 1,994

8) In the following right triangle, what is the value of x?
   A. 15
   B. 30
   C. 45
   D. 60
   E. It cannot be determined from the information given

6 cm

6 cm

9) What is 5 percent of 480?

    A. 20

    B. 24

    C. 30

    D. 40

    E. 44

10) In a basket, the ratio of red marbles to blue marbles is 3 to 2. Which of the following could NOT be the total number of red and blue marbles in the basket?

    A. 15

    B. 32

    C. 55

    D. 60

    E. 70

11) A square has an area of $81cm^2$. What is its perimeter?

    A. $28 \, cm^2$

    B. $32 \, cm^2$

    C. $34 \, cm^2$

    D. $36 \, cm^2$

    E. $54 \, cm^2$

12) Find the missing number in the sequence: 5, 8, 12, ..., 23

    A. 15

    B. 17

    C. 18

    D. 20

    E. 22

13) The length of a rectangle is 3 times of its width. If the length is 18, what is the perimeter of the rectangle?
   A. 24
   B. 30
   C. 36
   D. 48
   E. 56

14) Mary has y dollars. John has $10 more than Mary. If John gives Mary $12, then in terms of y, how much does John have now?
   A. $y + 1$
   B. $y + 10$
   C. $y - 2$
   D. $y - 1$
   E. $y + 3$

15) Dividing 107 by 6 leaves a remainder of
   A. 1
   B. 2
   C. 3
   D. 4
   E. 5

16) If $6,000 + A - 200 = 7,400$, then $A =$
   A. 200
   B. 600
   C. 1,600
   D. 2,200
   E. 3,000

17) For what price is 15 percent off the same as $75 off?
    A. $200
    B. $300
    C. $350
    D. $400
    E. $500

18) Which of the following fractions is less than $\frac{3}{2}$?
    A. 1.4
    B. $\frac{5}{2}$
    C. 3
    D. 2.8
    E. 3.2

19) Use the equation below to answer the question.
$$x + 3 = 6$$
$$2y = 8$$

What is the value of $y - x$?

    A. 1
    B. 2
    C. 3
    D. 4
    E. 5

20) If $310 - x + 116 = 225$, then $x =$
    A. 101
    B. 156
    C. 201
    D. 211
    E. 310

21) Of the following, 25 percent of $43.99 is closest to
    A. $9.90
    B. $10.00
    C. $11.00
    D. $11.50
    E. $12.00

22) Solve.
    8.08 − 5.6 = ….
    A. 2.42
    B. 2.46
    C. 2.48
    D. 3
    E. 3.2

23) If 500 + □ − 180 = 1,100, then □ = ?
    A. 580
    B. 660
    C. 700
    D. 780
    E. 900

24) There are 60 students in a class. If the ratio of the number of girls to the total number of students in the class is $\frac{1}{6}$, which are the following is the number of boys in that class?
    A. 10
    B. 20
    C. 25
    D. 40
    E. 50

25) If $N \times (5 - 3) = 12$ then $N =$?
    A. 6
    B. 12
    C. 13
    D. 14
    E. 18

26) If $x \blacksquare y = 3x + y - 2$, what is the value of $4 \blacksquare 12$?

    A. 4
    B. 18
    C. 22
    D. 36
    E. 48

27) Of the following, which number if the greatest?

    A. 0.092
    B. 0.8913
    C. 0.8923
    D. 0.8896
    E. 0.88

28) $\frac{7}{8} - \frac{3}{4} =$

    A. 0.125
    B. 0.375
    C. 0.5
    D. 0.625
    E. 0.775

29) Which of the following is the closest to 4.02?

    A. 4
    B. 4.2
    C. 4.3
    D. 4.5
    E. 3.5

30) Which of the following statements is False?

    A. $(7 \times 2 + 14) \times 2 = 56$

    B. $(2 \times 5 + 4) \div 2 = 7$

    C. $3 + (3 \times 6) = 21$

    D. $4 \times (3 + 9) = 48$

    E. $14 \div (2 + 5) = 5$

IF YOU FINISH BEFORE TIME IS CALLED, YOU MAY CHECK YOUR WORK ON THIS SECTION ONLY. DO NOT TURN TO OTHER SECTION IN THE TEST.　**STOP**

SSAT Lower Level Math Practice Tests Answers and Explanations

SSAT Lower Level Math Practice Tests Answer Key

SSAT Lower Level Math Practice Test 1				SSAT Lower Level Math Practice Test 2			
1	D	16	D	1	D	16	C
2	B	17	B	2	B	17	E
3	D	18	D	3	A	18	A
4	E	19	B	4	E	19	A
5	C	20	D	5	C	20	C
6	C	21	A	6	D	21	C
7	C	22	B	7	A	22	C
8	E	23	B	8	C	23	D
9	B	24	C	9	B	24	E
10	A	25	B	10	B	25	A
11	C	26	C	11	D	26	C
12	C	27	D	12	B	27	C
13	B	28	C	13	D	28	A
14	D	29	D	14	C	29	A
15	C	30	D	15	E	30	E

Score Your Test

SSAT scores are broken down by its three sections: Verbal, Quantitative (or Math), and Reading. A sum of the three sections is also reported.

For the SSAT lower level, the score range is 300-600, the lowest possible score a student can earn is 300 and the highest score is 600 for each section. A student receives 1 point for every correct answer. For SSAT Lower Level, there is no penalty for wrong answers. That means that you can calculate the raw score by adding together the number of right answers.

The total scaled score for a Lower Level SSAT is the sum of the scores for the quantitative, verbal, and reading sections. A student will also receive a percentile score of between 1-99% that compares that student's test scores with those of other test takers of same grade and gender from the past 3 years.

Use the following table to convert SSAT Lower Level Quantitative Reasoning raw score to scaled score.

SSAT Lowe Level Quantitative Reasoning raw score to scaled score

Raw Scores	Scaled Scores
Below 10	*Below* 400
$11 - 15$	$410 - 450$
$16 - 20$	$560 - 500$
$21 - 25$	$510 - 550$
$26 - 30$	$560 - 600$

SSAT Lower Level Quantitative Practice Tests Explanations

SSAT Lower Level Quantitative Practice Test 1

1) **Choice D is correct.**

   There are 10 squares and 6 of them are shaded. Therefore, 6 out of 10 or $\frac{6}{10} = \frac{3}{5}$ are shaded.

2) **Choice B is correct.**

   $\frac{12}{8} = 1.5$, the only option that is greater than 1.5 is $\frac{5}{2}$.

   $$\frac{5}{2} = 2.5 \,, 2.5 > 1.5$$

3) **Choice D is correct.**

   If $\frac{1}{3}$ of a number is greater than 8, the number must be greater than 24.

   $$\frac{1}{3}x > 8 \rightarrow \text{multiply both sides of the inequality by 3, then: } x > 24$$

4) **Choice E is correct.**

   $4 \times (M + N) = 20$, then $M + N = 5$. $M > 0 \rightarrow N \; could \; not \; be \; 5$

5) **Choice C is correct.**

   The closest to 5.03 is 5 in the options provided.

6) **Choice C is correct.**

The ratio of lions to tigers is 10 to 6 or 5 to 3 at the zoo. Therefore, total number of lions and tigers must be divisible by 8.

$$5 + 3 = 8$$

From the numbers provided, only 98 is not divisible by 8.

7) **Choice C is correct.**

A represents digit 4 in the multiplication.

$$14 \times 342 = 4,788$$

8) **Choice E is correct.**

N is even. Let's choose 2 and 4 for N. Now, let's review the options provided.

A) $\frac{N}{2} = \frac{2}{2} = 1, \quad \frac{N}{2} = \frac{4}{2} = 2,$ One result is odd and the other one is even.

B) $N + 4 = 2 + 4 = 6, 4 + 4 = 8$ Both results are even.

C) $2N = 2 \times 2 = 4, 4 \times 2 = 8$ Both results are even.

D) $(2 \times N) + 2 = (2 \times 2) + 2 = 6, (4 \times 2) + 2 = 10$ Both results are even.

E) $N + 1 = 2 + 1 = 3, 4 + 1 = 5$ Both results are odd.

9) **Choice B is correct.**

$8.9 - 4.08 = 4.82$, which is closest to 4.8

10) **Choice A is correct.**

The value of digit 5 in both numbers x and y are in the tens place. Therefore, they have the same value.

11) **Choice C is correct.**

$$5 + x = 20 \rightarrow x = 15 \rightarrow 15 + 25 = 40$$

12) **Choice C is correct.**

$$\frac{2 + 5 + 6 \times 1 + 1}{5 + 3} = \frac{14}{8} = \frac{7}{4}$$

13) **Choice B is correct.**

Area of a square = (one side) $\times$ (one side)

$$2 \times 2 = 4$$

14) Choice D is correct.
$$20 = x \times 4 \rightarrow x = 20 \div 4 = 5$$
x equals to 5. Let's review the options provided:

A) $x + 4 \rightarrow 5 + 4 = 9$ 20 is not divisible by 9.

B) $2x - 4 \rightarrow 2 \times 5 - 4 = 6$ 20 is not divisible by 6.

C) $x - 2 \rightarrow 5 - 2 = 3$ 20 is not divisible by 3.

D) $x \times 4 \rightarrow 5 \times 4 = 20$ 20 is divisible by 20.

E) $x + 1 \rightarrow 5 + 1 = 6$ 20 is not divisible by 6.

The answer is D.

15) Choice C is correct.

$$x - 12 = 18 \rightarrow x = 6$$
$$16 + y = 21 \rightarrow y = 5$$
$$x + y = 6 + 5 = 11$$

16) Choice D is correct.

$$\frac{5}{4} \times \frac{6}{2} = \frac{30}{8} = \frac{15}{4}$$

Choice D is equal to $\frac{15}{4}$.

$$\frac{5 \times 3}{4} = \frac{15}{4}$$

17) Choice B is correct.
$$5 + 3N = 41 \rightarrow 3N = 41 - 5 = 36 \rightarrow N = 12$$

18) Choice D is correct.
$$15 - 20 = -5$$
The temperature at midnight was 5 degrees below zero.

19) Choice B is correct.
Area of a triangle $= \frac{1}{2} \times (base) \times (height) = \frac{1}{2} \times 5 \times 8 = 20$

20) Choice D is correct.
$$area\ of\ a\ square = side \times side$$

 Side

21) Choice A is correct.

$$2 + 3 = 5 \rightarrow 5 + 4 = 9 \rightarrow 9 + 5 = 14 \rightarrow 14 + 6 = 20 \rightarrow 20 + 7 = 27$$

22) Choice B is correct.

$$average = \frac{sum\ of\ all\ numbers}{number\ of\ numbers} = \frac{6 + 10 + 12 + 23 + 45}{5} = 19.2$$

23) Choice B is correct.

There are 8 red ball and 20 are total number of balls. Therefore, probability that John will pick out a red ball from the basket is 8 out of 20 or $\frac{8}{8+12} = \frac{8}{20} = \frac{2}{5}$.

24) Choice C is correct.

An equilateral triangle has 3 lines of symmetry.

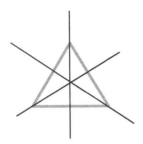

25) Choice B is correct.

10 percent of 200 = 10% of 200 = $\frac{10}{100} \times 200 = 20$

26) Choice C is correct.

Let's review the options provided:

A) $2 \times 2 = 4$ This is true!
B) $(4 + 1) \times 5 = 25$ This is true!
C) $6 \div (3 - 1) = 1 \rightarrow 6 \div 2 = 3$ This is NOT true!
D) $6 \times (4 - 2) = 12 \rightarrow 6 \times 2 = 12$ This is true!
E) $(10 + 23) \times 10 = 330 \rightarrow 33 \times 10 = 330$ This is true!

27) Choice D is correct.

The shape has 6 equal sides. And is side is 4. Then, the perimeter of the shape is:
$4 \times 6 = 24$

28) Choice C is correct.

$$\frac{4}{5} - \frac{3}{5} = \frac{1}{5} = 0.2$$

29) Choice D is correct.

$N = 2$, then: $\frac{64}{2} + 4 = 32 + 4 = 36$

30) Choice D is correct.

Four people can paint 4 houses in 10 days. It means that for painting 8 houses in 10 days we need 8 people. To paint 8 houses in 5 days, 16 people are needed.

SSAT Lower Level Quantitative Practice Tests Explanations

SSAT Lower Level Quantitative Practice Test 2

1) **Choice D is correct.**

$$\frac{8}{2} - \frac{3}{2} = \frac{5}{2} = 2.5$$

2) **Choice B is correct.**

$$48 = 3 \times N + 12 \rightarrow 3N = 48 - 12 = 36 \rightarrow N = 12$$

3) **Choice A is correct.**

There are 5 shaded squares. Then: $5 \times 8cm^2 = 40cm^2$

4) **Choice E is correct.**

$$\frac{x}{15} + 9 = 11 \rightarrow \frac{x}{15} = 11 - 9 = 2 \rightarrow \frac{x}{15} = 2 \rightarrow x = 15 \times 2 = 30$$

5) **Choice C is correct.**

$$3 + (4 \times N) = 23 \rightarrow 4N + 3 = 23$$

6) **Choice D is correct.**

78 divided by 5, the remainder is 3. 45 divided by 7, the remainder is also 3.

7) **Choice A is correct.**

$$2,400 - 606 = 1,794$$

8) **Choice C is correct.**

All angles in a triangle sum up to 180 degrees. The triangle provided is an isosceles triangle. In an isosceles triangle, the three angles are 45, 45, and 90 degrees. Therefore, the value of x is 45.

9) **Choice B is correct.**

$$5 \text{ percent of } 480 = \frac{5}{100} \times 480 = \frac{1}{20} \times 480 = \frac{480}{20} = 24$$

10) **Choice B is correct.**

The ratio of red marbles to blue marbles is 3 to 2. Therefore, the total number of marbles must be divisible by 5.

$3 + 2 = 5$

32 is the only one that is not divisible by 5.

11) **Choice D is correct.**

$$Area \ of \ a \ square \ = \ side \times side = 81 \rightarrow side = 9$$
$$Perimeter \ of \ a \ square \ = \ 4 \ \times \ side \ = \ 4 \times 9 = 36$$

12) **Choice B is correct.**

$$5 + 3 = 8, \quad 8 + 4 = 12, \ \ 12 + 5 = 17 \ , \ \ 17 + 6 = 23$$

13) **Choice D is correct.**

The length of the rectangle is 18. Then, its width is 6.
$$18 \div 3 = 6$$
$$Perimeter \ of \ a \ rectangle = 2 \times width + 2 \times length = 2 \times 6 + 2 \times 18 = 12 + 36 = 48$$

14) **Choice C is correct.**

$$Mary's \ Money = y$$
$$John's \ Money = y + 10$$
$$John \ gives \ Mary \ \$12 \rightarrow y + 10 - 12 = y - 2$$

15) Choice E is correct.

   Dividing 107 by 6 leaves a remainder of 5.

16) Choice C is correct.

$6,000 + A - 200 = 7,400 \rightarrow 6,000 + A = 7,400 + 200 = 7,600 \rightarrow A = 7,600 - 6,000$
$= 1,600$

17) Choice E is correct.

$75 off is the same as 15 percent off. Thus, 15 percent of a number is 75.

Then: $15\% \ of \ x = 75 \rightarrow 0.15x = 75 \rightarrow x = \frac{75}{0.15} = 500$

18) Choice A is correct.

$$\frac{3}{2} = 1.5 > 1.4$$

19) Choice A is correct.

$$x + 3 = 6 \rightarrow x = 3$$
$$2y = 8 \rightarrow y = 4$$
$$y - x = 4 - 3 = 1$$

20) Choice C is correct.

$310 - x + 116 = 225 \rightarrow 310 - x = 225 - 116 = 109 \rightarrow x = 310 - 109 = 201$

21) Choice C is correct.

   25 percent of $44.00 is $11. (Remember that 25 percent is equal to one fourth)

22) Choice C is correct.

$$8.08 - 5.6 = 2.48$$

23) Choice D is correct.

$$500 + \square - 180 = 1,100 \rightarrow 500 + \square = 1,100 + 180 = 1,280$$

$$\square = 1,280 - 500 = 780$$

24) Choice E is correct.

$\frac{1}{6}$ of students are girls. Therefore, $\frac{5}{6}$ of students in the class are boys. $\frac{5}{6}$ of 60 is 50. There are 50 boys in the class.

$$\frac{5}{6} \times 60 = \frac{300}{6} = 50$$

25) Choice A is correct.

$$N \times (5 - 3) = 12 \rightarrow N \times 2 = 12 \rightarrow N = 6$$

26) Choice C is correct.

If $x \blacksquare y = 3x + y - 2$, Then:
$$4 \blacksquare 12 = 3(4) + 12 - 2 = 12 + 12 - 2 = 22$$

27) Choice C is correct.

Of the numbers provided, 0.8923 is the greatest.

28) Choice A is correct.

$$\frac{7}{8} - \frac{3}{4} = \frac{7}{8} - \frac{6}{8} = \frac{1}{8} = 0.125$$

29) Choice A is correct.

The closest number to 4.02 is 4.

30) Choice E is correct.

$$14 \div (2 + 5) = 14 \div 7 = 2 \text{ not } 5$$

"Effortless Math" Publications

Effortless Math authors' team strives to prepare and publish the best quality Mathematics learning resources to make learning Math easier for all. We hope that our publications help you or your student Math in an effective way.

We all in Effortless Math wish you good luck and successful studies!

Effortless Math Authors

www.EffortlessMath.com

... So Much More Online!

✓ FREE Math lessons

✓ More Math learning books!

✓ Mathematics Worksheets

✓ Online Math Tutors

Need a PDF version of this book?

Please visit www.EffortlessMath.com

Made in the USA
Monee, IL
10 March 2021